Successful Pitching for Business In A Week

Patrick Forsyth

Patrick Forsyth runs Touchstone Training & Consultancy and has worked, widely and internationally, as a trainer specializing in marketing and communications skills. He writes extensively on business matters and is the author of many successful books for managers and executives, all designed to offer proven, practical guidance on all the skills required for job and career success.

Successful Pitching for Business In A Week

Patrick Forsyth

www.inaweek.co.uk

Also available in ebook

Contents

Introduction

Selling has never been easy and, especially in today's competitive conditions, can be downright difficult. What's more, some sales are inherently more challenging to achieve than others. The process of pitching – that is, multi-stage selling usually necessitating a formal presentation – is a case in point: every detail must be well executed if you are to maximize your chances of success. This book takes you step by step through every stage of the process so that you will gain confidence in your ability to pitch successfully.

Whatever your persuasive intention, and it may be pitching for a major contract or – sometimes equally difficult – putting an idea to your boss, the process is broadly similar. While agreement can, of course, sometimes be achieved at the end of one brief conversation, other circumstances will demand something more complex. It's not that you want to go through a more complex process but that the type of customer or client demands it.

The stages involved in the sales 'pitch' process usually start with a meeting: a briefing at which the client sets out (albeit with your assistance) exactly what they want. At that meeting you can respond and suggest how you might help. Very often they will want to see your considered view – your recommendations – in a written proposal. That delivered, you may then be asked to make a formal, 'stand-up' presentation, perhaps to a board, a committee or a buying department. This adds a new dimension and demands additional skills.

Even if the client decides in your favour, other discussions and follow-up may be necessary, to tie things down. To achieve further orders, even when the client or customer knows you and is satisfied with what you have already delivered, you may have to go through the whole process again. At every stage you may be pitching against others, so to be successful not only do you have to do it well but you must also do it better than your competitors.

Additionally, it's important to remember that such a process is *cumulative*. This means that each stage must be completed to the satisfaction of the other party or they will simply decline to go any further. If, for instance, you put in a bad, or even lacklustre, written proposal, you may never get the chance to go on to make a presentation. People will 'vote with their feet' and just go no further.

You will want to undertake the process in a way that will ultimately gain agreement, since failure can waste a good deal of time and money, so every stage must be managed in the right way and executed in the best possible manner. While the perfect pitch may rarely be achieved, luckily there are approaches and techniques you can use that will make success easier and more certain. This book sets out to show you the best way to proceed, to make the process manageable and to help you maximize your success, or 'strike rate'.

Patrick Forsyth

SUNDAY

Making a good start

To be able to pitch you need someone to whom to pitch. This may be someone in your own organization, your boss perhaps, or an existing customer or client, or someone you may need to find. Whoever your prospect is, you need to make a good start and a good impression and set the scene for the whole process. A key element is discovery: finding out exactly what people want. This chapter explores how to make this stage effective, and covers:

- the first conversation
- the first meeting
- how to find out what the client wants
- how to identify the client's needs and priorities.

The first conversation

Realistically, if someone approaches you or is recommended to you, it is likely that they will check you out a little. So your initial conversation with them needs to allow for this and for each party to find out more about the other. This is true if they telephone you or, perhaps later, if you meet with them. If you find that they have visited your website, for instance, don't assume that they have read and retained every word but do assume that they know something about you. Make sure that any detail you give about your organization flows on from, and is compatible with, the information on the website.

The art and science of pitching – and it is surely a mixture of both – are an added dimension to the art of persuasion and selling. (See *Selling In A Week* in this series for more on selling techniques, which are a necessary foundation to the pitching process.)

Even the earliest action in pursuing the sort of complex sales process reviewed here must not be taken in isolation. It must:

● respect and reflect the marketing and promotional activity that precedes it (as with the website just mentioned)
● become a formative part of what it is hoped will be an ongoing client relationship.

The progression of events is usually well anticipated in most fields that have sales complexity. And neither you nor the prospect expects a deal to be made in a moment. There are four main stages:

1 The initial contact confirms that a meeting is called for.
2 A meeting will start the process in earnest and allow you to discover further information.
3 A written proposal will explain and record your suggestions for how you, your products or your services can solve a problem, for instance.
4 As numbers of people are often involved on the client side, the next main step is often a formal presentation, when essentially the proposals are explained in more detail and questions answered.

After these main stages a good deal of follow-up action may be necessary, such as further meetings, before agreement is achieved. The whole process does not happen in five minutes, and often weeks and even months may go by before matters are concluded.

The first meeting

An initial briefing meeting is, of course, a sales meeting too, and everything about the way it is conducted must play its part in making the whole thing persuasive. What takes place must be acceptable and set the scene for the future. This first meeting must:

- inform both sides and do so clearly
- persuade
- differentiate your offer from the competition.

From the start, everything must be treated in a way that recognizes the likelihood of competition, so you should always ask about competition – 'Is this something you are talking to others about?' You will not always get a straight answer but you might. Even knowing one detail such as the number of other organizations that will pitch, or the size of a competitor relative to you, will help you.

The most important thing stemming from an initial meeting is information. You need to know exactly what they want, and you also need to know as much as possible about:

- the person or people you meet
- how the decision will be made
- the organization and whether its circumstances influence the decision in which you are involved (whether it is part of growth plans or retrenchment, for example).

There is also much to be learned about other matters such as timing, urgency, financial constraints and more – all of which can help you towards a successful outcome.

The crux of the initial meeting in terms of the pitch that follows is twofold: first the questioning and secondly the beginnings of setting out what you might offer.

 Ready, aim and fire!
This is a logical order of action for both the military and those in selling. If preparation equates with 'ready', then identifying needs is certainly likely to improve the aim. 'Fire', for the salesperson, means being 'on target': having a clear understanding of the client and relating what you offer to their specific and individual needs.

Winning pitches is by no means only about putting over your case. It demands not the 'gift of the gab' alone, but also the ability to ask questions, to do so in the right way, and to use the answers to better target the approach that you then deploy as you expound your case and make suggestions. Of course, your prospect will volunteer the answers to some of your questions, but perhaps only briefly or partially. Good investigative skills are necessary here.

What clients want

Clients have two prevailing feelings when buying or considering buying from a particular supplier:

● **They feel that they are the important one in the relationship.**
You sometimes hear salespeople talking about 'the buyer's support', as if there were some reason why people should do business with them just to help them. This is wrong. There is no reason in the world why clients should *support* you; they will *only* do business with you if *they* decide it is in *their* interests to do so. So they are right to see themselves as important, and the way in which you handle them in terms of courtesy, efficiency and appropriateness must reflect this.

● **They want a potential supplier to consider their needs.**
They consider their needs to be unique, if only in detail. Selling is usefully described as 'helping people to buy', which suggests strongly that having knowledge of what clients want, exactly what they want and how they want it, is the basis for sales success. Recognizing this principle actively helps you succeed. Of course, you have to find out exactly what needs a particular client has, and then use that knowledge to increase the effectiveness of your sales approach.

The gentle art of finding out

Despite your pressing need to find things out, questions must be asked carefully. This is true whether you are starting with a blank slate or whether a prospective client begins by stating a brief that is, in their view, clear. You should always check, clarify and, if the need and opportunity are there, extend their brief. This is because client briefs often change during the course of a discussion, and questioning in part prompts them to clarify or even adapt their thinking to a larger or smaller extent. Care is always necessary here because:

- most clients are busy, and do not want you subjecting them to a time-consuming or aggressive style of questioning; though with a major project in mind they may need little persuading that time spent on this process is necessary and worth while
- you need accurate information that will then help you differentiate yourself from your competitors. Certainly, knowing more than a competitor must help.

Asking good questions

How do you go about this questioning? There are several factors that will make what you do work well. Questions need to be:

- **accurately phrased**
  If a question is not clearly and precisely phrased, ambiguity may prompt the wrong answer.

- **mostly open-ended**
  Open-ended questions are those that cannot be answered by 'yes' or 'no'. Thus, 'Tell me exactly how you plan to use our services' is better than 'Do you see a cost advantage?' The first gets them talking (which is why open-ended questions work best) while the second, while it may be answered 'yes', may well leave other reasons for considering using you unsaid. Open-ended questions are likely to be the best way of getting what may well be the considerable amount of information you need, and are most likely to make the process acceptable to the client. Closed questions (those that can be answered 'yes' or 'no') can be used to vary the conversation and verify more specific details in checklist style.

● probing

Using a series of linked questions allows you to dig deeper and deeper to pursue a particular line and establish fuller understanding. This is an important technique and comprises four levels of questioning:

1 **Background questions** produce the basic detail, such as 'What kind of company is it?', 'How is this organized?' and 'What is its budget?' or whatever the required areas of information may be.

2 **Problem questions** (also called opportunity questions) are the first level of probing questions, which begin to explore what area of activity the product or service being reviewed is to fit in with. The problem need not always focus on something negative.

3 **Implication questions** further probe the points raised at the previous level to see exactly what the results of any purchase will be.

4 **Need questions** are the final set of questions and this is where you want to be – focusing on the need.

An example makes the principle clearer. Imagine the beginnings of a conversation between someone with a house to sell and a possible agent. Questions like 'How many rooms does it have?' 'Where exactly is it located?' and 'How long have you lived there?' are all background questions, and provide a useful start to the agent's information gathering.

Then a question like 'Are you aiming for a quick sale?' followed by 'Why is that?' takes things to the next level. Let us assume that the questioner discovers that the potential seller has a house to buy in mind and young children who would benefit from not missing the start of a new term at school in their new area. This is useful information and, if followed up by an implication question, 'Does this mean you can be a little flexible on price?', puts the questioner on strong ground.

Finally, a need question focuses the client's mind: 'So, if I could suggest a marketing plan that might work fast, but still maximize the price you get for your house, would that hit the spot?' If the estate agent can then do just that, suggesting a plan that sounds practical, the client will surely take notice.

The four phases of information gathering

Here's an example of a conversation between an architect and a potential client.

1 Background

Architect: What are your reasons for wanting to build on to your house?

Householder: I guess when we moved here we downsized a bit too much and we just need more space.

A: What kind of space exactly? What's it going to be for?

H: Well, the main thing is to create a study. There is a sort of computer corner in the living room, but it reduces the useful space in that room too much.

2 Problem

A: When we spoke, you mentioned that the extension should run off the living room but, now I see the room, mightn't that cause problems of access to the garden: out of the living room into the new study and then out to the garden?

H: I guess so; the double doors out from the study will take up most of the back wall and we also want a lot more shelves.

3 Implication

A: And you were talking about having a put-you-up bed in the study, weren't you? Might this just not create the space you want?

H: Yes, that could be.

4 Need

A: So, if we could position the new room so that access from the living room to the garden was still possible and extend the living room at the same time, would that be likely to give you the increase in space you want?

H: Well, yes, it would; what do you suggest?

Never skimp this finding-out process. If it is well done, it makes everything you have to do during the remainder of the selling process easier. And if you are in competition and find out the salient facts more accurately than anyone else, it can give you an edge over them throughout the rest of the process.

TIP

Clarify the brief
In many circumstances, your questioning is as much about clarifying a brief as it is about finding things out from scratch.

Listening to what the client says

> *'We have two ears and one mouth so that we can listen twice as much as we speak.'*
>
> Epictetus, Greek philosopher (c.55–135 CE)

Listening is always important throughout a meeting, especially when questioning is involved. You will look at least careless, and at worst incompetent, if you say something later during the process that makes it clear that you have not been listening properly to what a client has said. Listening is actually easier said than done; there may be many distractions and your mind is necessarily on a number of things at once: what to say next, what to ask and so on. You must listen carefully, *very* carefully, to everything the client says, and it must be apparent to the client that you are doing so.

Making notes

You can obtain a great deal of information in a short time with effective questioning techniques: too much to trust to your memory, however good you feel it is. You must make notes as you go along. The need for this is compounded by the fact that you often do not know in advance which bits of the plethora of information coming to light will be useful; the relevance of specific points may only become clear as matters progress. In some meeting situations it may be appropriate to ask for permission before writing down something a prospect says.

All this may seem very obvious, but many have walked out of a meeting and immediately had to ask themselves, 'What was it they said?' – so make notes.

Agreeing needs

Finding out what clients want, exactly what they want and why (and keeping a note of it) is essential. However, it is one thing for you to find out, and find out accurately, what your clients want; it is another for them to know that you have done so. Unless they are aware that you have an accurate picture of their requirements, they will never develop the same confidence in what you say or recommend. The usefulness of what you have discovered will be reduced.

The answer is to agree with the client that the needs are true reflections of what the client has said. This can

SUNDAY

MONDAY

TUESDAY

WEDNESDAY

THURSDAY

FRIDAY

SATURDAY

be done with further simple questions: 'Is that right? Am I understanding you correctly?' Alternatively, it can be done by summarizing: 'Let me just be sure I have got this right; what you are saying is...', listing the key points that have emerged. This makes sure you are correct, and it makes that accuracy of understanding clear to the client. It also allows you to refer back to points in the right sort of way when they are discussed again later in the conversation.

You will give a better impression to the client if you say something like 'This will give you the cost effectiveness you said was so important' when you refer to the way your product or service will suit them, than if you say: 'This will be cost effective, which I am sure you will appreciate.' In the latter case your own certainty may be justified – cost effectiveness is something most people want – but it may be unwise to make assumptions about more specific matters.

TIP Link what you say to client needs
Regularly use the client's words as an integral part of your conversation and description. This helps link what you say to their feelings and needs and so sharpens your sales effectiveness.

Two kinds of need

There are more client needs than the rest of the space in this book could list. Some are generic: many kinds of client want value for money, efficiency or to save money. Different clients may buy the same thing for very different reasons. For example, different people may choose the same holiday at the same resort for different purposes:

● to provide a romantic break or honeymoon
● to indulge in sporting activities
● to meet old friends, or make new ones

- to work quietly
- to impress the neighbours, or get away from them.

Reasons for choosing something (needs) may be tangible or intangible. You might buy a particular make of car in order to fit it into your garage (a tangible need for something less than a maximum size) or because it has good fuel economy (which can also be measured), or to meet a need to look successful or 'cool', both of which are more difficult to specify.

A key implication here for the pitching process is that intangible needs can be very important to people. However, they may be overlooked, or not taken seriously, by others who do not share the same needs or who do not understand them. When pitching, it's important to understand that intangible matters can become deciding factors when competitors are evenly matched and buyers are searching for something to help them make a final decision.

The buyer will assess the tangible factors, but if this only narrows their options down to, say, two possible contenders, they may well be influenced towards a final choice by something intangible. This might be something as vague as the overall image of an organization or of people, or something involving a subjective judgement. In conversation, if you recognize that this stage is being reached, then you must focus as much on the intangible as the tangible, perhaps exclusively so.

TIP

Don't overlook intangible needs
In taking steps to identify needs, intangible needs are often as significant as tangible ones, and information about both must be sought and the implications for the possible course of the conversation recognized.

Agreeing client priorities

Before the identification of needs stage is complete, you must ascertain something about clients' priorities. This is important because their various needs often seem straightforward but can, in fact, be in conflict. For instance, a client may say clearly that they want a service supplied:

- fast
- to a high quality
- at the lowest possible price.

Achieving all this may be unrealistic from any supplier; something available fast and of high quality will often be relatively expensive, and something less expensive may well take longer to supply. Which factor is, in fact, the most important? Superficially, the answer may be that all three criteria are important. Further questioning can discover that, if a choice has to be made, the client regards cost as the most important, or that timing is key and the client's attitude to cost will change to achieve what they want in this area.

How you proceed will be radically altered by such priorities: imagine, for instance, the differences posed for an estate agent when told to sell a property either at the highest possible price or as quickly as possible. Just as with needs themselves, the identified priorities can be agreed with the client and any reference back made in their terms: 'So, your priorities will be met, achieving completion ahead of that deadline and...'

SUNDAY

MONDAY

TUESDAY

WEDNESDAY

THURSDAY

FRIDAY

SATURDAY

As your product or service will be acceptable to the client only if it meets their priorities, this identification is crucial. Without it, everything else you do can be off target. If priority identification is achieved accurately, the case you go on to describe is then more likely to fit in neatly with their requirements.

Summary

Today you have learned that, when pitching, a good beginning sets the scene, demonstrates your professionalism and shows you are someone others can work with. The quality of the first conversation and the first meeting will influence the success of both the next stages of the pitch and the long-term relationship you may want to establish with your prospect.

It's vital to develop your skills in finding out what factors are important to your client, because good information informs everything you do in subsequent stages. Having better information than a competitor makes it easier to differentiate yourself from them in a positive way.

Get this stage right and you'll have taken a constructive first step towards achieving success. Tomorrow you'll learn how to use your brief from the client to plan and prepare your proposal, describing the course of action you'll take.

SUNDAY

MONDAY

TUESDAY

WEDNESDAY

THURSDAY

FRIDAY

SATURDAY

Fact-check [answers at the back]

1. How likely is a prospect to check you out before a meeting?
a) Slightly likely ❏
b) Very likely ❏
c) Not likely ❏
d) Highly likely ❏

2. What is the fourth major stage of pitching?
a) A lunch meeting ❏
b) A telephone call ❏
c) A formal presentation ❏
d) Written communication ❏

3. What characteristic underpins successful client communication?
a) Friendliness ❏
b) Pushiness ❏
c) Clarity of information ❏
d) Rapid response ❏

4. Should you ask the client about your competition?
a) Never ❏
b) Rarely ❏
c) Almost always ❏
d) Only if it is raised ❏

5. What's the most useful form of questioning?
a) Open-ended ❏
b) Hypothetical ❏
c) Closed ❏
d) Strident ❏

6. How is information gathering best done?
a) Fast ❏
b) Superficially ❏
c) Thoroughly ❏
d) Randomly ❏

7. How likely is success if you collect more and better information than your competitors?
a) More likely ❏
b) Less likely ❏
c) Certain ❏
d) Unlikely ❏

8. What should you accompany your questions with?
a) Smiling ❏
b) Telling anecdotes ❏
c) Taking notes ❏
d) Small talk ❏

9. What's the best way to treat clients?
a) As if they have all the time in the world ❏
b) As if they are busy ❏
c) As if they have few time pressures ❏
d) As if you don't know what time it is ❏

10. Having discovered needs, what do you then need to discover?
a) Their actual order of priority ❏
b) The client's personal preference ❏
c) Their A–Z order ❏
d) The total number of them ❏

MONDAY

Planning a powerful response

After the initial meeting with your client – one that as we have seen has the characteristics of a briefing – the next stage is to plan and prepare a proposal that sets out the way ahead. While nothing touched on here is intellectually taxing, and much will strike you as common sense, there are complexities, not least in orchestrating the entire process of pitching in a considered and systematic manner that will prompt action over whatever timeframe is necessary. The way you do this will influence how successful you are, so today you will learn the importance of:

- checking the brief
- making your pitch understandable
- making your pitch attractive
- making your pitch credible.

Why plan?

The sequence and the detail within the stages involved in pitching make it a fragile process. Opportunities for something to go wrong or simply be less effective than it might be are legion. However, while planning makes what needs to be done sound daunting and time consuming, it is no more than the age-old premise of engaging the brain before the mouth (or hands on keyboard in terms of a written proposal).

With a routine matter the plan may take only a few minutes. On the other hand, what needs to be done must be done, and if it takes a number of people talking it through for some hours to find and organize the best way to pitch for a substantial contract, then so be it. Preparation must never be incomplete if you are to maximize the chances of success.

Checking the brief

You will doubtless have notes from your meeting as to what the brief is you are addressing and also about suggestions already made, albeit perhaps in outline form. It is worth checking over these promptly when you are back at your desk to be sure they are clear; it is easy to make a quick note in a meeting and then fail later to see the exact relevance of it. Furthermore, if reviewing your notes alerts you to anything that was not clarified at the meeting, *now* is the time to go back and ask. Clients will not mind you checking to clarify a detail and it is easier early on to describe so doing as a request for additional information. Leave it and it becomes embarrassing because it can be more difficult to stop it sounding like inefficiency.

With a clear and complete brief stating what the client requires in front of you, there are several matters to consider before you decide a course of action and write a proposal to describe it:

- An initial review should give you **a general idea of the way ahead** (for example, as a trainer I might be asked to conduct a course to develop, say, presentational skills, and I'll need to think first about the kind of people it is for and their experience, what content should be included and what duration is appropriate).
- In some fields you need to think about your **people**: who will be involved in the project and whether consultation with them at this stage is necessary or useful; there might also be other people you can usefully talk to in order to pick their brains if they have more specific experience of something than you do.
- Some **research** (external or internal) may also be advisable; for instance, you may need to know more about the client's business, product or current circumstances.

With the full picture in mind, you can set out a plan describing your detailed suggestions – or recommendations – to the client. At this stage, if others are involved, it may be something that needs doing in tandem; indeed, roles may need to be allocated. The common difficulty of getting people together when all are busy must not be permitted to negate collaboration. A lack of co-ordination and understanding between those involved can dilute or destroy the chances of success later. The plan evolved or created will need to be written up clearly and appropriately in a formal proposal document if that is the next required stage.

Before turning to this task, the subject of Tuesday's chapter, you need to learn a core area of sales technique, one that must be reflected in all communications about the project and certainly in a written proposal. This concerns the way you describe your suggestions. As you work on the way forward and what will specifically be suggested, you need to bear in mind that everything must be expressed *understandably*, *attractively* and *credibly*.

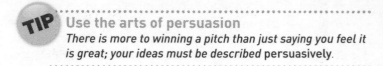

TIP Use the arts of persuasion
There is more to winning a pitch than just saying you feel it is great; your ideas must be described persuasively.

Making your pitch understandable

It is probable that more pitches are lost because of lack of understanding than for any other reason. The more complex the pitch you are describing, the greater is the danger of misunderstanding. Why? Because communication is not easy, especially between two people with different backgrounds, experience, intentions, prejudices and points of view. This may involve the different interpretation of one word – for example, just how fast is *immediately*? It could mean something sent quickly to arrive tomorrow or a phone call *now*. Alternatively, it may be that a long and disjointed explanation of, say, the cost advantages offered ends up confusing rather than informing the other party.

Therefore the first rule is to take care when putting across your message, and never assume that communication is entirely straightforward. Make sure that you choose words carefully and that you work at being clearly understood. Similarly, avoid repeating slavishly out of pure habit a standard version of a pitch that is not fully tailored to the present prospect. Remember, too, that people are really impressed by a good explanation: something that they expected to be complicated but which turns out to be straightforward. This is an excellent way of making a good impression, and of positioning yourself as professional.

Four other factors help guarantee that there is understanding:

1 Structure

The logic of any message is crucial. This means taking things one at a time, in bite-sized pieces that you can deal with manageably and that the client can comprehend, and flagging or 'signposting' what is being done.

Signposting

A pitch that begins, 'You will want to know something about how we can meet your needs, what costs are involved and how quickly things can be up and running. Let's take your needs first, then I'll say something about the finances, then...' is likely to be followed more easily than one where you just jump in and deal with points at random. If people know what's coming and feel it will be what they want to hear, they will be more receptive. Indeed, knowing that your initial thinking is clear and appropriate will impress them and give what is to come more credibility. The antithesis, the 'And another thing' approach, where what is expressed is apparently at random and unprepared, much less designed to be appropriate to the individual, is much less powerful and may fail to make your case.

2 Sequence

This goes logically with structure. Make the points of your message in a clear and relevant sequence (chronological, for example); what this sequence is should be made obvious to your audience. Every meeting needs thinking about and organizing in this way, to make sure that one, two, three does not become two, three, one.

3 Description

Your intention should be not just to tell people something but also to paint them a picture. It is essential that people *see* what you mean. You must stir their imagination. Here you must avoid bland language: no plan is just *practical* nor is it *very practical* – spell out what you mean by such statements and don't sell yourself short by failing to create a real picture in people's minds and thus not generate full understanding. Bland language can dilute the impression you want to give by default, and using it is not really a very good approach. Let me rephrase that: it is a disastrous approach that can kill the prospects of gaining agreement stone dead.

4 Visual aids

Something visual always makes things easier to understand; and this applies equally to a meeting, the proposal and to slides used in the presentation that may follow. A graph may make a point about cost effectiveness in a moment, when it might otherwise take many minutes to explain; photographs, charts and diagrams can all help you get your message over. See what is available. Create more if necessary, and use them.

> ### 'One picture is worth a thousand words.'
> Proverb

Check understanding

In presenting your case, being clearly understood is of paramount importance; understanding is the foundation upon which the rest of the selling process rests.

Beware of jargon

Nothing dilutes understanding more easily than inappropriate use of jargon. Jargon is professional slang and is particularly used in the context of technical matters. Between people of like understanding it is useful shorthand but jargon phrases must not be used externally or they will cause confusion. What is worse, you may not detect such confusion.

People do not always react at once to such a word or phrase. They do not pause and check what it means (not least because they may fear that they should know and do not wish to appear stupid). They let it go and hope that the overall sense will remain clear. However, if your words fail to make complete sense regularly, people will notice. If their understanding is reduced and they lose track of what you are saying, they will have to ask for clarification and will resent the need to do so. Either way, your credibility suffers. So watch out for jargon, especially as for most people its use is a habit. (If this is the case with you, become a recovering 'jargonaholic' as soon as possible.)

Jargon comes in two varieties: organizational jargon and industry jargon. Corporate jargon used within an organization often involves using sets of initials to describe products, systems, processes, people, departments and other things familiar to those within the organization and where a shorthand description is useful, provided everyone understands it. Certain industries can also give rise to technical jargon, some more than others. Computers are a case in point, one with which we are probably all familiar. Computer manuals are often a nightmare in their lack of clarity, mainly because of the jargon used, which, one assumes, was (wrongly) felt to be fine when the document was written.

As these examples show, the important thing with jargon is not so much to avoid all the technicalities but to make absolutely sure that they are pitched at an appropriate level for those individuals to whom you are speaking. In addition, some jargon phrases become so hackneyed that they lose all meaning. I once asked a friend in the computer world what exactly the phrase 'user friendly' meant. He thought for a moment, then said, 'I suppose it means it's very, very complicated, but not as complicated as next year's model!'

Once a handy phrase, it is now used in so many other contexts that it no longer has any real power and is thus somewhat past its sell-by date.

Making your pitch attractive

It is one thing to be understood, but quite another to make your descriptions truly attractive so that clients want to listen and are keen to let you complete the case. So how do you do this?

Talk benefits, not features

The basic principle here is that people do not buy products and services for what they are; they buy them for what the products or services do for them or mean to them – for their benefits. For example, people do not buy precision drills – what they are – but they buy the ability to make precision holes – what they do – and they will only want that because of some deeper need: to repair the car or put up shelves.

This is probably the single most important tenet of successful selling, yet the world over there are many people talking predominantly about features, when they should be talking about benefits. As a result, there are too many potential buyers, with their eyes glazing over, saying to themselves, 'So what?'

Talking benefits, and indeed leading with benefits, is important in making what you say attractive. It is not complicated, yet perhaps because you may have learned about what you sell from the starting point of a technical perspective, it is somehow more natural to talk about features. It can take conscious effort to state things the other way round.

The first task is to recognize which is which, feature or benefit, and it's useful to think through your product or service listing the benefits first and seeing how they link with the features. All the description you plan to use can be handled in this way. Look at each feature and say about it 'The feature is ... which means that...' and then develop the description so that it focuses on benefits and becomes both inherently more interesting and more closely linked to the actual need of the client.

Beware of short statements
Avoid the tendency to allow short statements to do the job of a better explanation; it's a very common way of allowing the power to persuade to be short-changed.

Feature or benefit?

A car may have a six-speed gearbox (a feature). Telling someone this may seem just like another piece of technical information, prompting the response 'So what?' Worse, an inexperienced driver may worry that it is more complicated than he or she can manage. If you as the salesperson have identified a need for economy, you can talk first about low fuel usage and money saved (benefits), quoting the feature of the six-speed gearbox as the reason that makes that possible.

One feature may, of course, link to more than one benefit. In the case of the car, reduced engine wear and smoother, quieter high-speed cruising may also result from the six-speed gearbox. Try thinking this through with something a little more technical in mind (ABS brakes or torque, perhaps for the car) or applying it to your own situation.

Talking benefits in this way, as you describe product, company, people and the services that support them, is a vital part of any pitch. It is worth a bit of thought – planning – to get it right.

Remember that all clients are different, and in some cases you may be selling to a group of people who *all* have influence

31

on a decision, as with a board of directors. In all cases, people will have their own needs and agenda, and benefits must be presented so that they relate to all these individual situations and points of view.

Relate benefits to individual clients

It's vital to tailor your approach to your particular prospect and this goes for the way you describe benefits. It's one thing to define what the various benefits or features are, but that does not mean you have to throw all the benefits indiscriminately at every client. Two things are important here: suitability and selectivity.

● **Suitability**
In the above example of a motorcar, fuel economy was shown as a benefit assisted by the feature of a six-speed gearbox (this is not the only contributor to the level of fuel use, of course). However, the usefulness of this benefit depends on the individual customer being interested in economy. Someone buying a high-performance, prestige car such as a Ferrari might well not care how far it goes on a litre of fuel, though they could be interested in other benefits produced by the same feature – high-speed cruising being more comfortable in a higher gear. So benefits must always be selected intelligently to match client needs and priorities.

● **Selectivity**
The amount that you could say about your organization, your people and your ideas is huge. It's easy to bore people. Comprehensiveness is never, or very rarely, an objective; achieving comprehensiveness just takes far too long. People are busy and they expect you to concentrate on what is most important – to them. You must have all sorts of information at your fingertips in terms of benefits, but you must select from your stockpile carefully, picking those benefits which you judge most likely to make the case you want, and then using them in the most succinct and logical way possible. Do this and your proposition will seem more attractive to more people.

Deploying different types of benefit

There are three different types of benefit and each presents different opportunities to make what you sell appear attractive. These are:

- **benefits to the person in their job;** here you need to stress the things that you are suggesting in terms of how they will make the work go well, or better
- **benefits to the client as a person,** stressing such factors as those allowing someone to justify a decision to buy to their boss
- **benefits to others who are important to the client,** such as their staff or customers.

The more you work with the concept of benefits, the more adept you will become at putting things in the terms with which clients most readily identify.

Time and care spent on getting the core description of what you sell right – focused on what it will do for the (individual) client – is vital. Without this, any description will risk seeming pedestrian and be unlikely to top competitive offerings; with it, you have an immediate competitive edge.

Making your pitch credible

The third element of the pitch to consider is how to make what you say convincing and credible to the client. Assume, first, that the client has some inherent scepticism towards anyone selling. They believe that you have a vested interest; they believe that they need to be sceptical and, if a good point is made about your product or service, their first reaction may be to think, 'They would say that, wouldn't they?' So they want proof.

The main form of evidence, certainly the one that builds in best to the benefit-oriented conversation you should be conducting, is the features. Well-selected benefits on their own reflect client needs. Benefits followed by features reflect needs and offer linked proof, as in a statement such as, 'This model will give you the low fuel consumption you want and reduce your motoring costs because it has a six-speed gearbox.'

There is factual, physical proof here: the client can see and touch the gear lever, and is reassured that it really exists and it is not just a sales ploy. Such proof may be asked for and, even if it is not, it should be built into the argument you are putting across, as it is an inherent requirement of the buyer. Never rely solely on your own argument; build some real proof into the case you present.

More proof may be needed than can be provided by features alone, and clients may demand that this comes from some outside, and preferably independent, source rather than the organization involved. For this reason it's a good idea to prepare a list of points that you can make in order to offer such external proof. There are different independent authorities to be quoted in different fields. For instance, all the following are sources of independent opinion and thus provide proof:

- an award received by your organization
- a link with another respected entity: a collaborator, perhaps
- sales figures and testimonials: match them to the people you are talking to so that they see them as compatible
- experience: 20 years in the business (and the time can be independently checked) may well mean something in terms of quality or reliability
- positive editorial comment in the trade press and other media.

You can probably think of more examples. Think systematically about your own organization, in order to assemble all possible proof factors that can be kept in mind and then used when appropriate. Have the right evidence ready and use it wisely.

Assemble your evidence

The right supporting evidence of all sorts, fielded in the right way, is powerful in adding credibility to your pitch and strengthening differentiation.

SUNDAY

MONDAY

TUESDAY

WEDNESDAY

THURSDAY

FRIDAY

SATURDAY

Summary

Recognizing that success starts with planning is the first step to achieving it. Pitching is a fragile process and must be got right and viewed correctly by everyone involved; indeed, organizing the roles of those involved is a key issue in itself.

First, you must be absolutely clear about the brief, checking it and clarifying anything about which you are unsure. Then you have to address the brief, designing a response to it: that is, exactly what it is you suggest and thus want to sell. The details of this must not just be described; they must also be put over persuasively. This means thinking about every point you will make so that it can be described clearly, seems attractive – an appropriate response to the brief that will give people what they want – and is also credible. The last may involve evidence, something more than just you saying that your offer is 'great'.

With this thought through, the next step is to put it down on paper, and it is to the task of writing an effective formal proposal document that we turn tomorrow.

SUNDAY

MONDAY

TUESDAY

WEDNESDAY

THURSDAY

FRIDAY

SATURDAY

Fact-check [answers at the back]

1. If anything about the brief proves unclear, how should you check it?
   a) By making assumptions ❏
   b) At the next meeting ❏
   c) Immediately ❏
   d) By guessing ❏

2. How important is planning a pitch?
   a) Essential ❏
   b) Advisable ❏
   c) Useful if time permits ❏
   d) Unnecessary ❏

3. How should you structure and sequence a pitch?
   a) By basing it exclusively on past pitches ❏
   b) Logically (to the client) ❏
   c) So that it's convenient to you ❏
   d) Randomly ❏

4. How should you use jargon?
   a) As little as possible ❏
   b) With care ❏
   c) As often as possible ❏
   d) By carefully matching it to the client's understanding ❏

5. What are benefits?
   a) Technical descriptions ❏
   b) Features of the product/service ❏
   c) Things that do something for the individual client ❏
   d) Background information ❏

6. In use, what should benefits relate to?
   a) You ❏
   b) Your organization ❏
   c) Your colleagues ❏
   d) The client's circumstances ❏

7. How many main kinds of benefit are there?
   a) One ❏
   b) Two ❏
   c) Three ❏
   d) Four ❏

8. What best enhances credibility?
   a) Detailed description ❏
   b) Third-party evidence ❏
   c) Repeating claims ❏
   d) Exaggeration ❏

TUESDAY

Putting persuasive proposals in writing

Once you are clear about the proposition you are going to put forward, you need to take it to the next stage. While not every client requires it, when it is necessary, written persuasion must be as good as that spoken face to face; and yet it is often weaker. Written proposals are very often a key part of the sequence of events: a good one takes things on down the sequence, while a bad one may stop progress dead in its tracks.

A proposal may be inadequate in just one small detail compared to another from a competitor, but that will be enough to place it second. Your proposal may be rated less impressive or appropriate by only a whisker, but you are still out. So the quality of written proposals is vital.

Today you will learn about:

- different types of proposal and their purpose
- how to decide what to include in a proposal
- how to structure your document
- how to write the covering letter
- the importance of the writing style and appearance of your proposal.

The nature of proposals

Proposals may vary. Some projects, such as a book proposal, for example, may be agreed after sending a page or two of text by email, while others may need substantial documents as part of the process of confirming a project. Whatever the size of your proposal, however, it must always follow the same set of principles.

If putting things in writing is not your stock in trade to the same extent as other aspects of your communication, it may be something you need to beef up. To be productive and successful, you need the ability not only to decide what to say, but to get words down in the right style and to do so quickly. You need to create powerful documents that inform, perhaps clarifying complex issues, that persuade – and that impress.

Quotations versus proposals

Proposals and quotations are terms that are sometimes used in a way that appears similar, but in sales terms they each imply something very different:

- **Proposals** have to describe, explain and justify what they suggest. They normally make recommendations (often bespoke ones), and they certainly should assume that their job is to persuade.
- **Quotations** are normally much simpler documents. They simply set out a particular – usually requested – option. They say that something is available and what it costs. They assume, rightly or wrongly, that the sales job is done and that persuasion is not necessary. This may sometimes be true, especially with repeat business. But many quotations should have more, sometimes much more, of the proposal about them.

Today you will be learning how to deal with the more complex of the two – proposals – though the principles concerned might also act to beef up any quotations you may use.

Choice of format

There are two main overall approaches to the format of proposals. Sometimes a letter, albeit maybe a longish one, is entirely appropriate. Indeed, sometimes doing more than this can overstate a case and put off the recipient. It may be seen as over-engineering, and sometimes as increasing costs. However, what is often necessary is something more formal that is like a report, though one with a persuasive bent.

The discussion document

This is a document for a stage before a proposal becomes appropriate. Its purpose is to set the scene for a meeting, describe the background, and define areas and ideas to be discussed at that meeting. Like all such documentation, the way it is written is vital to its success. A subsequent proposal is an extension of this discussion document.

Now consider both levels of formality in turn, and when and why each may be appropriate.

- **Letter proposal:** This is simply what the name suggests. It starts with a first sheet set out like a letter, beginning 'Dear...' It may be several pages long, with a number of subheadings, but it is essentially less formal than a report-style proposal. This style is appropriate when:
  - a more detailed proposal is not needed because there is insufficient content or less need for formality
  - the objective (or request) is only to summarize discussions that have taken place
  - there are no outstanding issues (unsolved at prior meetings, for instance)
  - there is no threat of competition.
- **Report-style proposal:** This is a report-style document, usually bound in some way and thus more elaborate and formal. This approach is appropriate when:
  - recommendations are complex
  - what is being sold is high in cost (or, just as important, will be seen as being so)
  - there is more than one 'client': this might be a committee, a recommender and decision maker acting together, or some other combination of people who need to confer and will thus see exactly the same thing

- you have not met everyone who will be instrumental in making the decision
- you know you have competition and are being compared.

How many copies of a proposal should I send?

The short answer is to ask the client and send however many are then requested. In many organizations it is common for there to be multiple decision makers or influencers. Where you even suspect that this is the case, it is doubly wise to ask how many copies of a proposal they need. If you have met, say, two people and the answer is three copies, this may indicate that there is someone else you need to be aware of and that there will be more questions (or even another meeting) before you can move on. Ideally, you have to find out what role the new person plays and make sure that the proposal addresses them as well as others.

Consulting the client

As always with selling, the client and their views rank high. What they want should rightly influence the kind of proposal you put in. Ask them questions, such as:

- How formal should it be?
- What sort of detail do they expect?
- How long should it be?
- How many people will see it?
- When do they want to receive it?

You do not have to follow their answers slavishly, but you must make a considered judgement. For example, if you are dealing with someone you know, they may well suggest not being too formal. However, if you know you have competition and the client is in discussion with other potential suppliers, it may still pay to set out something more formal than a letter; after all, your document and someone else's will be placed side by side and compared. In a comparison between a letter-style and more formal report-style proposal, the former tends to look weaker, especially when the client is considering the value-for-money element.

Timing

It is naturally good to meet client's deadlines, even if in some cases it means burning the midnight oil. However, it is likely that people will want your proposal to reflect your considered opinion. Promising that on a complex matter in 24 hours may simply not be credible. Too much speed in such a case can cast doubts on the quality and originality of the proposal, especially if you are in a consultative or advisory role or when solutions are positioned as being truly bespoke. In consequence, it may occasionally be politic to delay something, asking for more time than you actually need to enhance the feeling of tailoring and consideration when it arrives.

At this stage you know something about the client's needs, you know who is involved in the decision (i.e. those who will read whatever you write) and when the proposal is wanted. Remember the need for preparation: add in any time that composing such a document demands you spend with colleagues – in discussion, brainstorming or consultation – and set aside sufficient time to do a good writing job. Once the document is sent, then – for good or ill – it must stand on its own feet.

Proposal content and structure

While the form and certainly the content will vary, the structure of the proposal should usually have the following main sections:

1 title page
2 contents page
3 introduction
4 statement of need
5 recommendations (or solution)
6 costs
7 further details (such as timing, logistics, staffing and technical specification)
8 closing statement (or summary)
9 appendices (additional information such as technical detail that does not fit well elsewhere).

Each section may need a number of subsections with subheadings. The length of each section may vary with the context but having headed sections and then subheadings within them is a convenient way of signposting and highlighting the key issues within the proposal.

SUNDAY
MONDAY
TUESDAY
WEDNESDAY
THURSDAY
FRIDAY
SATURDAY

Make your headings interesting
The headings given in the list above are descriptive of the functions and role of the sections, not recommendations for the wording of headings you should necessarily use. It's best to choose headings that have impact.

Title page

A proposal of any complexity needs the equivalent of a book's title page. This states whom, or which organization, it is for, what it is about and who has produced it. This page can also give the contact details of the proposer (which, if not here, certainly must be somewhere in the proposal). Some people like to feature the logo of the recipient organization on it, as well as their own.

Contents page

Follow the title page with a sheet on which the contents of the proposal are listed and which gives the page numbers of each section. It may look more interesting if there are subheadings as well as main headings here, especially if the main headings have to be bland, for instance 'Introduction'. Better still, make sure the headings are not bland.

Introduction

Remember that a proposal is a sales document. The opening must command attention, establish interest and lead into the main text, making people want to read on. As the introduction has to fulfil a number of important yet routine tasks, it may be best to start with one or two sentences that are interesting, ring bells with the client and set the tone for the document.

Thereafter there are a number of other roles for the introduction. It may need to:

● establish the background
● refer to past meetings and discussions
● recap decisions made to date

- quote experience
- acknowledge terms of reference
- list the names of those involved in the discussions and/or preparation of the document.

Think, too, about how any necessary areas such as complaints procedure are expressed. As none of this is as interesting as what will follow (if it is, then you do have a problem!), this section should concentrate on essentials and be kept short. Its final words should act as a bridge to the next section.

Statement of need

This section needs to set out, with total clarity, the brief in terms of the needs of the client, especially if the client expects bespoke suggestions. It should describe the scope of the requirement, and may well act to recap and confirm what was agreed at an earlier meeting that the proposal would cover.

It is easy to ask why this section should be necessary. Surely the client knows what they want? Indeed, they have perhaps just spent a considerable amount of time telling you exactly that. But this statement is still important.

Its role is to make clear that you do have complete understanding of the situation. It emphasizes the identity of views between the two parties and gives credibility to your later suggestions by making clear that they are based firmly on the real – and, if appropriate, individual – needs that exist. Without this it might be possible for the client to assume that you are suggesting what is best (or perhaps most profitable) for you; or simply making a standard suggestion when they expect a tailored one.

This section is also of key importance if the proposal is to be seen by people uninvolved in the original discussions; for them, it may be the first clear statement of the situation. Again, this part should link naturally into the next section.

Recommendations

This may well be the longest section, and so to make it manageable you may need to divide it into smaller, logically arranged chunks. Clear and informative headings are essential. This is where you state what approach you feel meets the requirements. This may be:

- **standard,** in the sense that it is a list of, for example, recommended approaches that you have discussed and which you sell as a standard solution
- **bespoke,** as with the approach a consultant might take to a project, when the client wants a tailored solution.

In either case, this section needs to be set out in a way that is 'benefits-led', spelling out the advantages and making clear what the solution will mean to, or do for, the individual client as well as specifying the technical features. Thus don't just list what you will do, but also state what the result will be or how a stage will move things forward once completed.

Remember, the sales task here is threefold: to explain, to do so persuasively and also to differentiate you from the competition. A focus on the client's needs is usually the best way to gain the reader's attention; nothing must be said that does not have clear client relevance.

A particularly important aspect of your recommendations is that they must reflect the individuality of the client. It is so easy to store standard documents on disk and then to edit one proposal into a new version that does genuinely suit a similar need elsewhere, but you must double- and triple-check that you have changed the client's name and any other individual references. (One proposal recently sent to me called me

Margaret!) If a proposal is intended to look tailored, it must be just that and there must be no hint of it seeming standardized.

Only when you have completed this section of the proposal to your satisfaction should you move on to refer to costs, because it's only when the client appreciates exactly what value and benefits are being provided that they can consider costs in context.

Costs

All charges, costs or fees must be stated clearly, and not look disguised (though certain techniques for presenting the figures are useful, for example amortizing costs – describing something as £1,000 per month rather than £12,000 for the year – and describing and costing stages separately).

All the necessary detail must be there, including any items that are:

- options
- extras
- associated expenses.

These must be shown and made clear.

Leaving aside details of marketing and pricing policy, note the following points when stating costs.

1 Link prices as closely as possible to benefits.
2 Establish or reinforce that you offer value for money; don't just state figures baldly.
3 Include invoicing details and trading terms, where relevant; mistakes here tend to be expensive (for the UK, remember to make clear whether price includes VAT).

4 For overseas clients, pay attention to currency considerations.
5 Make comparisons with the competition or with past projects.
6 Use range figures (necessary in some kinds of business)
   with care: do not make the gap too wide and never go over
   the upper range figure.

Might not some people turn first to costs? Yes, without a
doubt this happens – indeed, it is only realistic to assume that
some readers will look at this page or pages before reading
anything else. This is why you need to include sufficient
explanation, cost justification and, above all, clear benefits,
linked in here. Just the bald figures can be very off-putting.
This section must not only deal with its discrete topic, but it
must also act to persuade any reader who starts here that
it is worth turning to the front and reading through from the
beginning. Write it to achieve just that, and remember that you
want it to be essentially a positive message: one of providing
value for money linked to meeting a brief.

 Link costs to benefits
*Make sure you arrange the costs section of your proposal
so that it is not just about facts and numbers – it must be as
persuasive as any other part of the document.*

Further details

It may be necessary to deal with additional topics here, as
mentioned above. These topics include timing, logistics and
staffing (for services). Sometimes they are best combined
with costs within one section if there are not too many of
them. For example, costs and timing go well together, and
then you might perhaps have one other separate, numbered
subsection dealing with any final topics before moving on.

The principles here are similar to those for handling costs.
Matters such as timing must be made completely clear and all
possibilities of misunderstanding or omission avoided.

Again, bear in mind the need for individuality and a
customized approach. For instance, a biographical note about

you and your colleagues, important in many services, needs to be tailored to any specific proposal where those actually involved in the work are a factor affecting decisions to buy. Never use standard CVs here, but adapt them to highlight aspects of each person's experience and so on that will be seen as desirable by that specific client.

Closing statement (or summary)

The final section must act to round off the document and has a number of specific jobs to do. Its first, and perhaps most important, task is, of course, to summarize the rest of the content. All the threads must be drawn together and the most important aspects emphasized. It fulfils a number of purposes:

- It is a useful conclusion for all readers and should ensure that the proposal ends on a note that they can easily agree is an effective summary.
- It is useful, too, in influencing others around the decision maker, who may study the summary but not go through the whole proposal in detail.
- It can ensure that the final word, and the final impression, left with the reader is about benefits and value for money.

 Write an effective summary
Because the closing statement or summary can often be the most difficult part of the document to write, it can thus make a disproportionate impression. Readers know good summarizing is not easy and they respect the writer who achieves it. It is a sign of professional competence.

In addition, the closing statement can be a useful place to:

- recap key points (as well as key benefits)
- stress that the proposals are, in effect, the mutual conclusions of both parties (if this is so)
- link to action, action dates and details of contact (though this could equally be dealt with in the covering letter)

- invoke a sense of urgency (you will normally hope for things to be tied down promptly, but ultimately need to respect the prospect's timing).

A conventional summary appears at the end of the proposal, but a so-called executive summary may be placed at the start of the document to do much the same job as one at the end. In part, it is a matter of taste or what the client has asked for, and sometimes you may want to include both. Having a traditional summary (at the end) is usually best for the decision maker, who will want to read the whole document before coming to the summary. For recommenders or others less involved, the executive summary may be preferred. Whichever you choose, it must be well written, and remember that a short final conclusion will still be necessary even when the main summary is placed at the beginning of the document.

 If in doubt, ask the client
If in doubt, ask your client whether they want an executive summary as well as or instead of a closing statement.

Appendices

It is important that proposals, like any document, flow. The argument they present must proceed logically and there must be no distractions from the developing picture. Periodically, there may be a need to go into deep detail but, especially if this is technical, tedious or involves numerous figures – however necessary the content may be – it is better not to let such elements slow and interrupt the flow of the overall argument. Such information can usefully be referred to at the appropriate point, but with a note that the detail of it appears in an appendix. Be specific, saying for example: 'For more information, see Appendix 2: Costs and timing, on page 21.'

Appendices can be used for a variety of elements: from terms and conditions to details inherent in the project. They can also be the place to put visual elements (for example the photographs or plans an architect may use to exemplify what they say). Careful consideration is needed here, not only about where to put things but also what to use as illustrations. When including illustrations, whether in an appendix or within the main part of the document, make sure you link them to what is being said and almost always insert an explanatory caption.

The covering letter

Your proposal should always be sent with a covering letter. In part it is a courtesy, yet the content of the letter is important, and all the more so for more complex situations and more elaborate proposals. It will, if it is interesting, be the first thing to be read. It sets the scene for the rest of the message and can usefully project something of the personality of the writer. This is why it must say more than 'Here is the promised proposal' (a compliments slip could do that): it is a useful place to add emphasis, perhaps instilling a sense of urgency, to touch on results or to set the scene for a future follow-up meeting.

The writing style

The writing style of both your proposal and your covering letter must be crystal clear, flow logically and be easy to read; it must be articulate and must not drift into the clichéd world of 'business speak', replete with unexplained jargon, overlong words and sentences, poor punctuation and grammatical and spelling mistakes. People may twitch at something as simple as the phrase 'forward planning' (planning is sufficient; you cannot plan the past!). Two actions are indicated here:

1 Check your writing over carefully, watching four (*sic*) errors that a computer spellchecker will not spot (e.g. check/cheque).
2 Let someone else read it.

 Brush up your writing skills
Be honest with yourself: if your writing style is insufficient to the task, take action to improve it. Go on a course, read a book on the subject, and have a dictionary, a thesaurus and a grammar guide to hand.

A shortfall in the quality of the writing, particularly alongside a better-written competitor, can lose you a sale. Some people equate poor grammar with a lack of care, experience or professionalism and hate to see obvious errors: for example, nothing can be very unique (unique means unlike anything else and cannot be qualified). Any detailed grammar advice is beyond the brief here, but the following boxed paragraph of (not entirely seriously phrased) examples will perhaps act as a reminder of the importance of this factor.

Some memorably put writing rules

- Don't abbrev things inappropriately.
- Check to see if you any words out.
- Be careful to use adjectives and adverbs correct.
- About sentences fragments.
- Don't use no double negatives.
- Just between you and I, case is important.
- Join clauses good, like a conjunction should.
- Don't use commas, that aren't necessary.
- Its important to use apostrophe's right.
- It's better not to unnecessarily split infinitives.
- Only Proper Nouns should be capitalized. also a sentence should begin with a capital and end with a full stop.
- Use hyphens in compound-words, not just in any two-word phrase.
- In letters, proposals and things like that we use commas to keep a string of items apart.
- Watch out for irregular verbs that have creeped into your language.
- Verbs has to agree with their subjects.
- A writer mustn't change your point of view.
- A preposition isn't a good thing to end a sentence with.
- Avoid clichés like the plague.

The appearance

A good appearance will not make up for bad writing, but it is important in its own right. Proposal documents need to look good, be neatly bound and reflect certain practical considerations too, such as:

- a binding that allows the document to lie flat
- a legible typeface – not too small
- sufficient white space (to allow the reader to add notes and annotations)
- clear headings and page (and, if appropriate, paragraph) numbering
- including illustrations that are relevant and captioned clearly.

Additionally, do not overdo the bells and whistles: colour, symbols and other such devices can improve appearance, but too many can result in things just looking a mess.

Summary

Too often a written document like a proposal can be a weak link in the pitching process. If it's bland it will dilute the case it tries to make, and if it's obtuse it will be difficult to follow and apt to confuse. If it is poorly written it will convey a lack of professionalism.

Today you have learned how to make sure your written proposals excel. Doing this takes time and care, from the first stage of thinking through the brief and making your proposition clear, to structuring and writing the proposal and the covering letter. The timing of it must be appropriate, it must fulfil any promises made, and the content and organization of it must be logical and clear. The whole thing must look good, read well and, above all, be seen to address the brief in a well-tailored manner, thus leading your client to take matters to the logical next step.

That next step is a presentation, and Wednesday's chapter tells you how to prepare a formal presentational pitch.

SUNDAY
MONDAY
TUESDAY
WEDNESDAY
THURSDAY
FRIDAY
SATURDAY

Fact-check [answers at the back]

1. When is a quotation better than a proposal?
   - a) When time is short ☐
   - b) When the client is busy ☐
   - c) Only when certain criteria are met ☐
   - d) If you want to conserve paper ☐

2. What should the proposal's style and form most closely link to?
   - a) Your convenience ☐
   - b) What's quickest to prepare ☐
   - c) The client's taste and requirements ☐
   - d) Past proposals ☐

3. How many copies should you send?
   - a) One ☐
   - b) Two ☐
   - c) Three ☐
   - d) Whatever people ask for when questioned ☐

4. How do appendices increase ease of reading?
   - a) By extending technical detail ☐
   - b) By labelling certain material unimportant ☐
   - c) By separating important detail from the overall flow ☐
   - d) They don't ☐

5. When should a proposal be delivered?
   - a) By a specified date ☐
   - b) As soon as possible ☐
   - c) When time permits ☐
   - d) At a time that reflects both client and internal objectives ☐

6. When should you use a covering letter?
   - a) Never ☐
   - b) Sometimes ☐
   - c) If asked for ☐
   - d) Always ☐

7. How should costs be described?
   - a) As briefly as possible ☐
   - b) In a way that links them to value for money ☐
   - c) In a way that disguises them ☐
   - d) In a way that confuses the reader ☐

8. What should the 'statement of need' section of a proposal do?
   - a) Remind the client of what they want ☐
   - b) Make the proposal comprehensive ☐
   - c) Fit expectations of style ☐
   - d) Show that *you* understand the brief ☐

9. What contribution does correct grammar make to a good proposal?
   - a) Very little ☐
   - b) None at all ☐
   - c) It depends on the client ☐
   - d) More than enough to make careful checking vital ☐

10. How important is it to check what you have written?
   - a) Unimportant ☐
   - b) Not at all, as it's done by the computer ☐
   - c) So essential that it should be done at least twice ☐
   - d) Only to be done if time permits ☐

WEDNESDAY

Preparing a formal presentational pitch

Now that you have spent time preparing your proposal, it is more important than ever to maintain the momentum of events. The later in the pitching sequence a potential client decides to opt out, the more money and effort are wasted.

The next stage is therefore equally important. Making a presentation is not easy and certainly few people, no matter how experienced, can do a good job of the task without some preparation. In the pitching process this involves:

- refining the proposal and seeing how it can be delivered in 'presentation style'
- thinking about who will do what
- deciding on the manner in which you will deliver the presentation
- choosing what visual aids you will need.

Today we look at how to get set to tackle all this so that you are ready to make the presentation.

The link between proposal and presentation

In many cases you will send your proposal in the hope that it will prompt a presentation. Once in front of the prospect, proposals, whether posted or emailed, must do their work alone, although you may want to follow this up in numerous ways: by letter, email, telephone and so on (persistence here can pay dividends).

Sometimes the link between proposal and presentation is less straightforward. For example, the client may want the presentation to come first and a proposal document to be based on the presentation.

Consider how to send your proposal

The emailing of a proposal can be satisfactory, especially if you need to send something quickly and you are dealing with people you know well (or if asked), but it does not put something as smart as a bound document on their desk. Speed may be of the essence sometimes, but you can always follow up an email with a hard copy sent physically.

You may know in advance that a complex proposal, especially one that will have more than one person making the decision, will be the subject of a formal presentation within the client organization. These can happen in two main ways:

1 The proposal is sent, then a presentation is made later to those who have (or should have!) read the document.
2 The presentation is made first, with the detailed proposal being left as a permanent reminder of the presentation's content.

Whichever arrangement you have made in advance, the wording and style of the proposal needs to reflect this. For example, you may need more detail in a proposal that has to stand on its own than one that follows a presentation. It might sometimes be possible (with the prospect's agreement) to delay completing the proposal until after a presentation;

this allows you to include any final elements stemming from feedback arising from the presentation meeting. Alternatively, you can issue a revised version at this stage, either amending or adding an appendix.

Certainly, there should be a close parallel between the two entities so that it is clear how anything being said at a presentation relates to the proposal, though rarely should it be read out verbatim. What is usually most important is for you to give additional verbal explanation of what has been written.

It may cause confusion if, say, a proposal with eight main headings is discussed at a meeting where nine or ten items are run through (certainly if this is done without explanation). It is helpful if you can make sure that the jobs of preparing the proposal and the presentation overlap and are kept close.

A further idea here may be useful: more than one company I know print out – for themselves – a 'presentation copy' of the proposal in a larger than normal format or type size. This enables it to be easily referred to by someone standing in as they give a presentation at a meeting. It also provides space for additional notes that will help the delivery of the presentation to go more smoothly. Just remember that page numbers will be different on the different versions and do not let this cause confusion.

TIP Understand the nature of the presentation
Check that you understand the nature of the sequence of events and the role of the proposal in relation to the allied presentation, because this will influence how the proposal is written.

Preparing your presentation

You will probably have worked out the case you will make in your presentation, having already encapsulated it in the written proposal, but you must now decide exactly what you will say and how you will put it over to your audience. Technology can be a mixed blessing, and one downside is that a common result is that the automatic response of someone due to give a presentation is to use a program like PowerPoint to produce electronically generated slides. The temptation then is to rely on the slides to the detriment of the presentation itself.

'Death by PowerPoint'

We are probably all too familiar with what has become known as 'death by PowerPoint': a presenter showing too many slides, slides with too much text on them and, at worst, the presenter reading verbatim from the slides – while looking away from their audience at a screen.

This does not impress and must be avoided. Slides should support what is said and much (most?) of the impact should come from what the presenter says and how they say it. Otherwise, why have a presenter at all? Reading from slides hardly puts over an image of professional competence and, besides, people read to themselves seven times faster than you can read out loud, so the whole thing can easily become disjointed.

Before addressing specifically how to get a presentation together in a way that will make it work, you need to know how long your presentation needs to be, where it will be held and the role of everyone taking part.

Duration

How long will your presentation be? You need to know. Nothing is more off-putting than arriving at a client's office all prepared and ready to deliver 45 minutes of deathless speech to be immediately told, 'Please keep it within half an hour; we have a tight schedule today.'

You need to ask about, discuss and agree duration in advance (and may still need to be a little flexible on the day). Then you can prepare something that fits the client's vision of how long it should take, though you may need to negotiate a little if they suggest so short a time that it will be difficult to do your case justice.

You will usually find that you have to think carefully about what you can include, rather than straining to fill the time. But any case must have sufficient weight in order to persuade. Just one reason, however beguiling, may fail to do the trick. Some interesting research (Nick Oulton, 2007) seems to confirm this, suggesting that five is the optimum number of main benefits needed to make success most likely. That does not mean that four or six are wholly inappropriate; taken as a guide to what gives a case significant weight, four to six main points seems about right. The research relates to businesses making formal presentations as part of what they do to produce business, so here the point makes particular sense.

Make sure you include all the main benefits
Whatever the time pressures, make from four to six main points in your presentation to ensure that the weight of your case is sufficient.

Venue

It also helps to know where the meeting will be held. Again, you can ask, perhaps at an initial meeting, and if you are told the actual location, ask to see it. It won't always be possible to see it beforehand but, if you can, it can prevent you later finding yourself in a room half the ideal size, unable to swing a cat and balancing papers on your knee as you struggle to look halfway competent.

A particular consideration here is equipment. Will you bring a computer or a memory stick? Will they provide a projector? And – most important – will their equipment and yours work together compatibly? I have seen more than one presentation proceed without slides because the computer of one party would not attach to the projector of the other.

If you know the environment in which you will be speaking, this will make you feel more comfortable. For example, I find that if I know there will be a table at the front of the room, a large, hard briefcase set on it will allow my notes to sit at a level where I can read them comfortably without bending or straining to see. On the day little details, like making sure you know where electric leads are so that you don't trip, and having a glass of water to hand, all make for a more comfortable and thus confident speaking experience.

The team

Everybody involved must know their role. Who will speak first, second and third? Who will introduce the session and who will act as its overall chair? Handover must be smooth – seamless – if several speakers are involved.

The job and the individual's presentational skills will dictate who is involved and what their role is. We all know of some senior managers who, in terms of the organization's hierarchy, should take part, or go first, but who should not be allowed within a thousand miles of a presentation. Ban them (or train them) but do not let hierarchical decisions dilute the quality of what is delivered on the day.

Each individual taking part may prepare their own section (and their own slides), but it makes good sense to have an 'editor in chief' to pull everything together and make sure it forms a cohesive whole and will be the right overall duration. Their word should be law.

Preparing the content

A presentation should have a clear objective. Anything delivered as just 'about something' is likely to be lacklustre. Here the objective is clear: you want to win the business or gain acceptance for an idea, and it is likely that you intend that action will follow (the client agrees, signs on the dotted line and you deliver). As you begin to put a presentation together, you need to know exactly what your aim is. For example, the best outcome immediately after the presentation may be for matters to be referred to the Board, for a test arrangement of some sort to be tried or more details supplied.

As you prepare the content (what will be said), any visuals that will support it must also be prepared. While these two things are closely related, it is the content that takes priority.

First, think through the content that is already set out in the written proposal and make notes on how you will present it. For example:

- What will you say?
- How much detail will you go into?
- What will you emphasize, explain further or illustrate?
- How will you enliven it, making it interesting, exciting, entertaining even?
- How can you do all this and still make it persuasive?

With practice, this need not be difficult. You will get to know what is best presented in the form of slides as a help to those listening and a reminder to you (though remember that their first purpose is always for the audience; don't show them things that are merely a memory jogger for you).

Initially, you may want to have a systematic and thorough way of going through this, as set out below. This method may precede writing the proposal as well as being used at this stage. With time and familiarity, this can be abbreviated, but make sure that you do not take short cuts that dilute the quality of what you will present.

The method has six stages. The best way of connecting the principles described here to real life is to go through them with a personal project of yours in mind, one related to a pitch you must make.

Stage 1: Listing

Forget about sequence, structure and arrangement for now; just concentrate on and list – in short note (or keyword) form – every significant point that the presentation might usefully contain. Give yourself plenty of space, perhaps using something larger than a standard A4 sheet so that you can see everything at a glance. Drawing from the proposal and your thoughts and discussions, set down the points as they occur to you, almost at random across the page. For something simple this might result only in a dozen words, or it might be far more.

You will find that this is a good thought prompter. It enables you to fill out the picture as one thought leads to another, with the freestyle approach removing the need to pause and try to link points or worry about sequence. With this done – and with some presentations it may only take a short time – you have a full picture of the possibilities for the message in front of you and you can move on to the second stage.

Stage 2: Sorting

Now you can review what you have noted down and begin to bring some order to it. Look at each item and decide:

- what comes first, second and so on
- what items logically link together, and how
- what provides evidence, an example or an illustration of the points you will make.

At the same time, you can – and probably will – add additional items and have second thoughts about others, which you will delete. You can also amend the wording a little if necessary – with an eye on the duration involved.

This stage can often be completed in a short time by simply annotating and amending the first-stage document. Using a second colour makes this quick and easy, as do link lines, arrows and other enhancements of the original notes.

At the same time you can begin to catch any more detailed elements that come to mind as you go through (including ways of presenting as well as content), noting what it is at more length on the page, or alongside it.

Stage 3: Arranging

Sometimes, at the end of stage two, you have a note that remains sufficiently clear and from which you can work directly to finalize matters. If it can benefit from clarification, however, it may be worth rewriting it as a neat list; or this could be the stage where you type it up on screen, if you are working that way and want to be able to print something out in due course, especially where a team is involved.

Final revision is possible as you do this. Certainly, you should be left with a list reflecting the content, emphasis, level of detail and so on that you feel to be appropriate. You may well find that you are pruning a bit to make things more manageable at this stage, rather than searching for more content and additional points to make.

Stage 4: Reviewing

This stage may be unnecessary if you have brought sufficient thought to bear through the earlier stages. However, for something particularly complex or important (or both) it may be worth running a final rule over what you now have written down. Sleep on it, perhaps, as a way to avoid finalizing matters for the moment, especially if you have got too close to it. It is easy to find you cannot see the wood for the trees.

Make any final amendments to the list (if this is on screen, it is a simple matter) and use this as your final 'route map' as preparation continues.

Stage 5: Preparing the 'message'

This means assembling each speaker's notes (dealt with in the next section) and the slides in the order that will form the material from which you speak. This is where you turn your firm intentions about content into something representing not only what will be said, but also how you will put it over. One of the virtues of the procedure advocated here is that it stops you trying to think about what to say and how to say it at the same time; it is much easier to take on each task in turn. This fifth stage must be done carefully, though the earlier work will have helped to make it easier and quicker to get the necessary detail down in the way you want.

Stage 6: Final checking

A final look (perhaps after a break) is always valuable. This is also the time to consider rehearsal. Either talk it through to yourself, into a tape recorder or in front of a friend or colleague, or go through a full-scale rehearsal as described below. If further revision is necessary to get it right, so be it.

Visual aids

Perhaps the most important visual aid is you, the presenter. A large number of factors, such as simple gestures like hand pointing and more dramatic ones like banging a fist on the table, which may be described as flourishes, are part of this, as is your general manner and appearance.

More tangible forms of visual aid are also important. Visual aids often mean slides, of course, but that's not all. Practically anything can act as a visual aid, from another person (carefully briefed to play their part) to an exhibit of some sort. In a pitch, exhibits may be obvious items such as products, samples, posters and so on, or may be something totally unexpected. Like all the skills involved in making presentations, while the basics give you a sound foundation, the process is something that can benefit from a little imagination.

Such things as props and slides can serve several roles, which include:

- focusing the attention of the audience
- helping change pace and add variety
- giving a literally visual aspect to something
- acting as signposts to where within the structure the presentation has reached
- providing reminders for the presenter, over and above their notes, of what comes next.

Whatever visual aids you choose, make sure that you pick those that are fit for purpose.

As already mentioned, it's important to be careful with slides and to make sure they *support* the message, not lead it or take it over. Just because slides exist or are easy to originate does not mean they will be right. You need to start by looking at the message, at what you are trying to do, and see what will help put over that message and have an additive effect. Slides may make a point that is difficult or impossible to describe in another way – a graph, for example, makes an instant point that would otherwise be lost in flurry of figures. Or you may have a particular reason to use them: to help get a large amount of information over more quickly, perhaps.

The checklist that follows offers some useful rules for using what is today the near-ubiquitous PowerPoint. Breaking these rules can seriously dilute your effectiveness.

Top tips for preparing slides

- Keep the content simple.
- Restrict the amount of information and *especially* the number of words on each slide:
  - use single words to give structure, headings, or short statements
  - keep slides uncluttered and simply laid out
  - use a running logo (e.g. the main heading or topic on each slide).
- Use diagrams, graphs and charts where possible rather than too many figures; and never read figures aloud without visual support.
- Build in variety within the overall theme, using colour or variations of the theme used.
- Emphasize the theme and structure, e.g. by regularly reusing a single slide to recap the agenda or objectives.
- Ensure that the content of any image matches the words.
- Make sure all content is necessary and relevant.
- Ensure that everything is visible, asking yourself:
  - Is it clear?
  - Is the typeface big enough?
  - Will it work in the room?
  - Does it suit the equipment?
- Ensure that the layout emphasizes the main meaning (and not some minor detail).

 Avoid slide distraction
You don't have to have a slide showing all the time. When you have finished with a slide it will start to distract people, so blank out the screen (with PowerPoint you just press 'B') until you are ready to use the next slide (at which point you just press 'B' again).

When using slides during the presentation, remember to talk to the group and not to the visual aid. Looking at the screen too much when slides are used is a common fault. Make sure visuals are visible (do not get in the way yourself), explaining them or their purpose as necessary. Finally, to stop people taking unnecessary notes and missing what is said, tell them that they will get a paper copy of the slides after the presentation, if this is the case.

Beware gremlins

Is this one of Murphy's laws? Certainly, it is an accurate maxim that if something can go wrong it will; and nowhere is this truer than with equipment.

The moral: check, check and check again. And remember that while the sophistication of equipment increases all the time, so too do the number of things that can potentially go wrong with it.

The concept of contingency is worth a thought; what will you do if disaster does strike? You have been warned.

Documents

Part of your preparation involves having the right documents with you, and the relationship between things here also needs to be right. You will need:

● **The proposal**
This may come in several forms: that originally sent, an expanded version to distribute after a presentation, and a 'presenter's copy' in larger type.

● **Your notes and papers**
You may wish to have your own set of notes to accompany your slides. There may also be other additional papers used on the day that do not form part of the proposal document.

● **Handouts**
Handouts might comprise printed copies of all the slides or just a selection of pages and charts from the slides,

designed to be studied up close, or pages from the proposal that had too much information to simply turn into slides.

Everything must be clear, legible and suitable for how it is used and there may usefully be several versions of things. For example, a graph may need to be shown. In the proposal or in a handout it may be quite detailed, but a slide of it may well need to be simplified or turned into two or more slides.

The rehearsal

There can be a good deal hanging on a pitch – the value of business at stake may be substantial. Yet often there is no rehearsal, and then mistakes occur. It's never easy to get people together, but the time it takes to run through most such presentations is modest compared with the task of replacing business lost, as it were, by default if a presentation fails to impress. It's therefore always a good idea to run through it in its totality and ask these questions:

- Does it flow?
- Is everything logical, clear and descriptive?
- Does it fit within the planned duration?

It's sensible to schedule this rehearsal so that you have plenty of time between it and 'the day'; you may find that you need to review, alter and improve the actual content. Indeed, you may find that you need more than one rehearsal, but it will be worth it.

Summary

Preparation is a vital part of communicating. At its simplest it takes merely moments of constructive thinking, but usually more than this is necessary. Key principles are always to precede any thought process by devising a clear objective and to prepare your messages with a firm idea of what intentions they reflect (informing, persuading, etc.).

If you think matters through systematically – separating the decision of *what* you will say (or put across) from *how* you will say it – you can choose the precise language and emphasis you will use. It's important to give this process sufficient time and, if possible, build in some pauses so that you can reflect on your work clearly and do not become unable to see the wood for the trees. Be prepared to fine-tune the message to get it right.

Tomorrow you will learn how to put all your preparation to good use when you carry out the on-the-day, on-your-feet delivery of your presentation.

SUNDAY
MONDAY
TUESDAY
WEDNESDAY
THURSDAY
FRIDAY
SATURDAY

Fact-check [answers at the back]

1. How should you connect a presentation to the proposal?
a) Keep them separate ❏
b) Design it carefully to link to the proposal ❏
c) Ignore the proposal document ❏
d) Only make some reference to the proposal document ❏

2. How much time should you spend on preparing a presentation?
a) Little time if you are experienced ❏
b) It's only a matter of rearranging existing slides ❏
c) It can be done at the last minute ❏
d) Time that must be sufficient and well ahead of the event ❏

3. What makes a poor start to preparing?
a) Writing 'Good morning' and proceeding from there ❏
b) Making tea ❏
c) Clicking automatically into PowerPoint ❏
d) Delaying ❏

4. How long should our pitch presentation be?
a) 20 minutes ❏
b) 30 minutes ❏
c) 45 minutes ❏
d) A duration agreed with the client ❏

5. How should any presentation team work?
a) To fit in with everyone's diary ❏
b) Without anyone 'in the chair' ❏
c) Just before the event ❏
d) Closely and in good time ❏

6. How should you prepare a presentation?
a) Systematically ❏
b) On the back of an envelope ❏
c) No need; I can wing it ❏
d) As time allows ❏

7. How should you view projection equipment?
a) As reliable ❏
b) As a support ❏
c) As the technician's problem ❏
d) Something to check carefully ❏

8. Which is true?
a) Slides can be packed with words ❏
b) Not all the information needs to be legible ❏
c) Only legible and relevant information should be on slides ❏
d) A 12-point type for words is fine ❏

THURSDAY

Making the presentation

Few people can speak in front of an audience without thought. Practice helps and so too, as we have seen, does preparation. Both preparation and execution need to be undertaken with an eye on the 'shape' of a presentation and how it should be arranged in order to achieve its objectives on delivery.

Today we examine that arrangement in terms of both the overall shape and the role of particular parts, and how to make every aspect of your presentation effective. We will look at the best ways to:

- manage your nerves
- structure your pitch
- gain your audience's attention and achieve rapport
- answer questions
- prepare your speaker's notes.

Managing your nerves

'It usually takes me three weeks to prepare a good impromptu speech.'

Mark Twain, writer (1835–1910)

Many people find making a presentation awkward, or even traumatic, at the best of times, and even more so when a great deal hangs on a pitch. This is natural. Being prepared makes it easier (for instance, if you have good notes and are familiar with them, then you will not lose your place), and so does taking a deep breath before you start, making sure you have a glass of water to hand and not having downed a double whisky to calm your nerves. Beyond that, you should:

- give your hands something to do, if need be (hold a pen)
- pitch your voice naturally to the back of the room
- keep a sharp eye on the timing.

All that is necessary for many apparent problems is a practical response, something that acts decisively to remove or reduce the adverse effect. Thinking of your presentation this way helps, too. Try not to worry: no doom and gloom. It will be more likely to go well if you are sure it will, and even more so if you work at organizing yourself. Confidence will aid you by projecting authority. So does a focus on your audience.

Your audience

Everything is easier if you have a clear idea of your audience. First, who are they? They may be people you know or strangers, experts in your field or inexperienced about the proposals you will put to them. Whoever they are, they will all have certain common expectations that you must address. Specifically, any audience will want you to:

- 'know your stuff'
- look the part
- respect them, acknowledging their situation and their views
- discover links between what you say and what they want from the pitch (they are looking for it to help them make a considered decision)
- give them an adequate message so that they understand and can weigh up whether they agree with what is said or not
- make it 'right for them' (for example, in terms of level of technicality)
- hold their attention and interest throughout.

What audiences *do not want* is to be:

- confused
- blinded with science, technicalities or jargon
- lost in a convoluted structure (or because there is no structure at all)
- made to struggle to understand inappropriate language
- made to struggle to relate what is said to their own circumstances
- having to listen to someone who, by being ill prepared, shows no respect for the group.

A good presenter will always have empathy for the group they address, and this must show clearly. Often this is something guided by prior knowledge. But sometimes you will not know people well. Always find out what you can and make use of everything you do discover.

Everything you do must reflect all this, and even seemingly small details matter. For example, your appearance and your personal organization have visual importance. Professionalism is, at least in part, inferred from appearance, and you must not just be well organized, you must *look* well organized. Walking to the front, however confidently, is likely to be spoiled if you are clutching a bulging folder spilling papers in all directions, and start by saying, 'I'm sure I have the first slide here somewhere', accompanied by fevered fumbling attempts to find it.

The structure of a presentational pitch

Probably the most famous of all maxims about any kind of communication is the old saying, 'Tell 'em, tell 'em and tell 'em.' That is, you should:

● tell people what you are going to tell them
● tell them
● then tell them what you told them.

This may sound simplistic, perhaps, but keeping to these three points when structuring your presentational pitch will help you focus and stay on track. Compare it with the way a good report is set out, for instance. There is an introduction, which says what it is that follows; there is the main body of the document, which works its way progressively through the message; and finally there is the summary, which says what has just been covered. The idea is straightforward, but if it is ignored, messages may go largely to waste.

The following guidelines follow this three-part structure, splitting the presentation into three sections. You will see not only how to make each section effective, but how to ensure that the three together make a satisfactory whole. Running through all of this, as already mentioned, should be the sound foundation of a clear purpose and thorough preparation.

The beginning of the pitch

The beginning is clearly an important stage for your audience. People will be expectant but uncertain about what is in store; they are wondering what the pitch will be like and whether they will find it interesting or helpful. They may also have their minds on other matters: what is going on elsewhere, the job they left half finished or the staff coping alone. This is particularly true when people either do not know you at all or don't know you well. They will have little or no previous experience of what to expect, and this will condition their thinking. With people you know well there is less of a problem, but the first moments of the presentation are nevertheless always important.

The beginning is also important to the presenter because nothing settles the nerves better – and even the most experienced speakers usually have a few qualms early on – than making a good start. The beginning is, necessarily, the introduction; the main objective is therefore to set the scene, state the agenda (and the rationale for it) clearly, and begin to discuss the 'meat' of the content. In addition, you have to obtain the group's attention – they will never take the message on board if they are not concentrating and taking in what is going on – and create some sort of rapport between you and the group, and also within the group itself.

Gain attention

attention - grabbing

This is primarily achieved by your manner and by the start you make. You have to look the part; your manner has to say 'This will be interesting, this person knows what they are talking about.' Certainly, if your start appears hesitant, the wrong impression will be given and everything thereafter will be more difficult. Therefore what you say first and how you say it is important.

There are a number of types of opening, each presenting a range of opportunities for differing lead-ins. You could start with any of the following:

- **A question:** This could be rhetorical or otherwise, and preferably something that people are likely to respond to positively. 'Would you welcome a better way to...?'
- **A quotation:** This might be humorous or to make a point. It might be a classic or novel phrase or something said by a colleague. 'At the last meeting, the MD said...'
- **A story:** Again, this could be something that makes a point, relates to the situation or people, or draws on a common memory. 'We all remember the situation at the end of last year when...'
- **A factual statement:** This could be a striking, thought-provoking, challenging or surprising fact. 'We are told that this company receives 1,200 calls from customers every working day.'

- **A dramatic statement:** Try a story with a startling end, perhaps, or a statement that surprises in some way.
- **An historical fact:** You could refer back to an event that is a common experience of the group. 'In 2011, when sales for what was then a new product were just...'
- **A curious opening:** Make a statement sufficiently odd for people to want to discover what on earth it's all about. 'Consider the aardvark, and how it shares a characteristic of some managers...' (In case you want the link, it's thick skinned.)
- **A checklist:** Perhaps placing a shopping list in mind early on is important. 'There are seven key stages to the process we want to discuss. First...'

No doubt you can think of more methods and combinations of methods to use. Whatever type of opening you select, this element of the session needs careful preparation.

 Make your first slide count
Try to avoid the much-used standard, rather bland and predictable, title slide that does little more than present the name of the speaker.

Create rapport

Right from the start, you need to ensure that you create an appropriate group feeling. In terms of what you say, you may want to set a pattern of using the word 'we' rather than 'them and us'; in other words, say, 'We need to consider...' and not 'You must...' Using this approach will help create a more comfortable atmosphere, and so will adding – discreetly – a compliment or two ('As experienced people, you will...'), though without being patronizing. Above all, be enthusiastic. It is said that the one good aspect of life that is infectious is enthusiasm, so use yours.

At the same time, the opening stages need to make it absolutely clear what the objectives are, what will be dealt with

85

and how it will benefit those present. It must also move you into the topic in a constructive way.

The middle

The middle is the core of your pitch. This is where you:

- put over the detail of the case
- ensure acceptance of the case
- maintain attention throughout the process.

You also need to anticipate, prevent and, if necessary, handle any possible objections.

One of the principles here is to take one point at a time; we shall do just that here.

Put over the content

The main trick here is to adopt a structured approach. Make sure you are dealing with points in a logical sequence: for instance, working through a process in chronological order. Use 'flagging' or 'signposting' of your points but keep it simple: don't say, 'There are three key points here; performance, method and cost; let's deal with them in turn. First, performance...' because that would be too much detail.

Just give advance warning of what's coming, in terms of both content and the nature of what you will say next. Saying 'For example...' is a simple form of signposting, which makes clear what you are doing and that you are not moving on to the next content point just yet. Putting everything in context, and relating it to a planned sequence, keeps the message organized and improves understanding.

This technique, and the clarity it helps produce, will give you the overall effect you want. People must obviously understand what you are talking about. There is no room for verbosity, for too much jargon, or for anything that clouds understanding. One pretty good measure of a presenter is when people afterwards feel that, perhaps for the first time, they really have come to understand clearly something that has just been explained.

Keep it simple

You cannot refer to manual excavation devices; in presenting, a spade has to be called a spade. What's more, it has, as it were, to be an interesting spade if it is to be referred to at all and if attention is to be maintained.

Maintain attention

Here again, the principles are straightforward.

● **Keep it relevant**

Keep stressing the relevance to the audience of what is being discussed. For instance, do not say only that some matter will be a cost saving to the organization, but stress the personal benefits – showing how it will make something easier, quicker or more satisfying to do, perhaps.

● **Keep visual interest**

Make sure that the presentation remains visually interesting throughout, with good visual aids.

● **Tell stories**

Use descriptions that incorporate stories or anecdotes to make the message live. You cannot make a presentation live by formal content alone; you need an occasional anecdote, or something less formal. It is good if you are able to both proceed through the content you must present and seemingly remain flexible, apparently digressing and adding in something interesting, a point that exemplifies or makes something more interesting as you go. How do you do this? It is back to preparation.

● **Be enthusiastic**

Continue to generate attention through your own interest and enthusiasm in your subject.

Obtain acceptance

The first step to acceptance is understanding. If they cannot understand your message, your audience will be unable to accept it as sensible. To aid understanding:

● use clear, precise language – language which is familiar to all those present, and which does not overuse jargon
● make explanations clear – making no assumptions, using plenty of similes (you can hardly say 'This is like...' too often), and with sufficient detail to get the point across. One danger here is that in explaining points that you know well, you start to abbreviate, allowing your understanding to blind you to how far back it is necessary to go with people for whom the message is new
● demonstrate your product or service – talk specifically about the products, for instance, and show one if possible. In this case, the golden rule is (surprise, surprise) preparation. Your credibility is immediately at risk if something is mentioned and needs visualizing, yet cannot be. Help your audience's imagination and you will get your message over better
● use visual aids, as already mentioned; these are a powerful aid to understanding.

As vital as understanding is, your ultimate aim is to get acceptance. Acceptance is helped by the factors already mentioned (telling people how something will benefit them or others they are concerned about, such as their staff), and the more specifically you do this the better the effect will be on the views formed. It is not enough to have put your message over and for it to be understood; it has to be believed. Nothing will be truly accepted unless this is achieved.

People will agree only with what they have come to believe is good sense, so realistically acceptance may come only once credibility has been established, and this, in turn, may demand something more than you merely saying that something is right. As discussed in yesterday's chapter, you need to provide evidence.

 Check for acceptance
You won't, of course, always know whether acceptance of a point has been achieved until later. Keep an eye on the visible signs, watching, for instance, for nods, smiles or puzzled looks and, if necessary, adjusting your delivery accordingly.

Handle objections

The first aspect here is the anticipation, indeed the pre-emption, of objections. On occasions it is clear that something about your pitch is likely, even guaranteed, to produce a negative reaction. If there is a clear answer, then it can be built into the presentation, avoiding any dilution of the case.

You may find that you can make a simple comment such as 'Of course, this needs time – always a scarce resource – but once set-up is done time will be saved', and then go on to explain how this will happen. Of course, objections may come as questions (during or after the presentation) – handling those is dealt with later in the chapter.

The end

Always end on a high note. The group expects it, if only subconsciously. It is an opportunity to build on past success during the session or, occasionally, to make amends for anything that has been less successful.

The end of your presentation should be a pulling together of the overall message that you have given, when you touch on key issues and aim to make the session memorable. There is often a need to summarize the content in an orderly fashion – completing the 'Tell 'ems' – and then seeking a commitment as to what should happen next. This is important because it makes it much more likely that something will happen, especially if follow-up action is taken to remind people to see the matter through.

Signing off

There are several ways to handle the final signing-off. In the same way that you gained attention at the beginning of the presentation, you might finish with any of the following:

- **A question:** This leaves the final message hanging in the air, making it more likely that people will go on thinking about the issues a little longer. 'I asked a question at the start of the session; now let's finish with another...'
- **A quotation:** This should encapsulate an important, or the last, point. 'As Neils Bohr said, "Prediction is difficult, especially of the future."' It can be linked either to the topic or to the occasion.
- **A story:** This has the same sort of intention as a quotation. It does not have to be amusing, but if it is meant to amuse, be careful and be sure it does; you have no further chance to retrieve the situation.
- **An alternative proposal:** This might be as simple as 'Will you do this or not?' or a more complicated set of options such as a spelled-out plan – 'Will you do A, B, or C?'
- **An extra 'carrot':** This is an injunction to act immediately, linked to an advantage of doing so now. 'If we can go ahead promptly, we can guarantee completion by...' More fiercely phrased, it becomes a fear-based end: 'Unless you ensure that this system is running, you will not...' Although there is sometimes a place for the latter, the positive route is usually better.

However you decide to wrap things up, the end should be a logical conclusion rather than something separate added to the rest of the pitch. By this stage every intention you had – creating rapport, informing, motivating, persuading, changing attitudes, demonstrating, illustrating and more – should have been achieved.

Answering questions

However good your presentation, you must take questions in your stride. The first thing to think about is how you will control this part of the pitch, although whoever is in the chair may dictate the format.

A presentation may be followed by a question-and-answer session, or you may prefer to take questions as you go. Decide this beforehand and say something about questions and how and when you will take them at the beginning of your presentation. If you take questions as you go, it makes control and timing more difficult, so don't be afraid to hold a question over ('We will come to that in a moment; perhaps I can comment then?') or to ask for more time ('I'm happy to take questions, but – [addressing the Chair] – how do you want to deal with this in terms of time?')

Leave time at the end for a final word from you. If you finish your presentation by simply saying 'Any questions?' and then get some, you may find them petering out, with the Chair saying, 'That seems to be all…' and concluding the session. It's better to reserve time for a final comment: 'We are pleased to take questions, but perhaps I could reserve a couple of minutes at the end to summarize.' This allows you to conclude in a punchy way – on a memorable note.

Most questions can probably be anticipated, and thus planned for. Even if they are not, deal with them succinctly and clearly, and bear in mind the following:

- If you are part of a team, decide which of you will answer which question.
- Take your time. No one will mind if you acknowledge something – 'That's a good point; let me think…' – as long as you give a good, considered answer.

- Be prepared to say you don't know. You can promise to check and get back to the questioner, but anything is better than uncertainty, waffle or an answer that loses its way.

Overall, as with many skills, the difficulty here is less with the individual elements, most of which are straightforward and common sense, than with the orchestration of the whole process. All those involved in the pitch must be able to present effectively, to remain flexible throughout, and ensure that this stage is completed successfully and powerfully.

TIP Be prepared for questions
Always plan for this part of your pitch: you can rarely, if ever, 'just wing it'. A badly run Q&A can undermine your message, while care in both preparation and execution can bolster your message and increase your audience's trust in you.

Your speaker's notes

For most people, having notes in front of them as they speak is essential. The purpose of speaker's notes is to:

- boost confidence: in the event you may not need everything that is in front of you, but knowing it is there is, in itself, useful
- act as a guide to what you will say and in what order
- help you present in the best possible way: helping produce the right variety, pace, emphasis and so on as you go along.

On the other hand, notes must not act as a straitjacket and stifle all possibility of flexibility. After all, your audience's interest might suggest a digression or the need for more detail before proceeding. Alternatively, the reverse might happen if a greater level of prior information or experience becomes apparent, meaning that you want to recast or abbreviate something you plan to say. It's also possible, as you get up to speak for 45 minutes, that the person in the Chair whispers, 'Can you keep it to 30 minutes? We are running a bit behind.' Good notes should assist with these and other scenarios as well.

When considering what form exactly they should take, there is no one right style. You must experiment and find something that suits you. However, a consistent approach will get you preparing more quickly and more certainly. The following rules and tried-and-tested approaches may help.

1 **Legibility is essential.** Use a sufficiently large typeface, or writing, avoid adding tiny, untidy embellishments and remember that notes must be suitable for use standing up and therefore at some distance from your eyes.
2 **Choose materials that suit you.** Some people favour small cards, others larger sheets. A standard A4 ring binder works well, and one with a pocket at the front may be useful for ancillary items you may want with you. Whatever you choose, make sure it *lies flat*. It is disconcerting if a folded page turns back on itself and you find yourself repeating a whole section. It has happened!
3 **Use only one side of each sheet of paper or card.** This allows space for any necessary amendments and additions and/or makes the total package easier to follow (some people like notes arranged with slides reproduced alongside or slotted in to keep everything together).
4 **Always use page numbers.** If you drop your papers – and one day you will – you can put them back in the right order. You may like to number the pages in reverse order – 10, 9, 8, etc. – to give you some guidance regarding the time remaining until the end, but stick with one way or the other to avoid confusion.
5 **Separate different types of note.** For example, separate visually *what* you intend to say from *how* (emphasis and so on).
6 **Use colours and symbols.** These will help you find your way; they will also serve to minimize what needs to be noted down.

Keep your notes as notes
Never put down verbatim what you want to say. Reading something is difficult and always sounds less fluent. The detail on the speaker's notes needs to be just sufficient for a well-prepared speaker to be able to work from it and do so comfortably.

Making your notes clear

Copy the following ideas for notes or adapt them to your own situation, adding any additional ideas that you think will suit you.

- **Main divisions:** Divide the pages – imagine they are A4 – into smaller segments (a coloured line is best), each creating a manageable area on which the eye can focus with ease; this helps to stop you losing your place (effectively it produces something of the effect of using cards rather than sheets).
- **Symbols:** These save space and visually jump off the page, making sure you don't miss them. It's best to avoid possible confusion by always using the same symbol to represent the same thing, and to restrict the overall number used. Examples of symbols are bold exclamation marks and a large 'S' followed by a number to indicate a slide.
- **Columns:** These separate different elements of the notes. Clearly, there are various options here in terms of numbers of columns and what goes where: slides, for example, can be indicated either within the text or on the left-hand side of a double-page spread.
- **Space:** Turning over only takes a second (often you can end a page where a slight pause is necessary anyway), so give yourself plenty of space, not least to facilitate amendments and, of course, to allow individual elements to stand out.
- **Emphasis:** This must be clearly shown in the content; again, a second colour helps.
- **Timing:** An indication of time elapsed (or still to go) can be included as often as you find useful; remember that most people like keeping to time commitments exactly.
- **Options:** These are points (separated in a discrete column) to be added or omitted from the presentation depending on such factors as time and feedback. They help fine-tune the final delivery and are also good for boosting confidence. A plan might thus include ten points under options, with half of them taking your total presentation up to the planned duration. Thus you can extend or decrease the content of your pitch to order, fluently working in additional material where more detail, an aside or an extra example seems appropriate on the day.

Summary

For a presentation, good preparation, good notes and good execution go together: the first two allow the third to happen. The structure of a presentation is not difficult or complicated: a beginning, a middle and an end are all it takes. What is necessary is to create and execute each part so that it fulfils its various purposes.

You usually get only one crack at a presentation, so if it's lucklustre or deficient in even just one small way, especially if that way is important to the client, the situation may not be recoverable and agreement may not be gained. Equally, it's true that every stage of the process, indeed practically every description, phrase or word you use, is an opportunity to impress – to increase just slightly the overall feeling for what you do – and ultimately to win the business. Being well prepared, sure of your material and confident also that you have a really clear guide in front of you will see you well on the way to making a winning presentation.

SUNDAY

MONDAY

TUESDAY

WEDNESDAY

THURSDAY

FRIDAY

SATURDAY

Fact-check [answers at the back]

1. How should a presenter appear to the audience?
   a) Fashionable ❑
   b) Casual ❑
   c) Stressed ❑
   d) Professional ❑

2. What relationship with your audience should be visible?
   a) Contempt ❑
   b) Fear ❑
   c) Empathy ❑
   d) Lack of interest ❑

3. How many parts should your presentation fall into?
   a) Four ❑
   b) Five ❑
   c) Three ❑
   d) Two ❑

4. What should the beginning of a presentation do?
   a) Start slowly ❑
   b) Gain people's attention ❑
   c) Make people check their watch ❑
   d) Induce sleep ❑

5. Which aspect of how you project is contagious?
   a) Tone of voice ❑
   b) Enthusiasm ❑
   c) Mannerisms ❑
   d) Pace ❑

6. How should your points be made?
   a) At random ❑
   b) In a logical order ❑
   c) Chaotically ❑
   d) Without differentiation ❑

7. What's the primary purpose of slides?
   a) To help the presenter keep track ❑
   b) To distract from the speaker's weaknesses ❑
   c) To support and highlight key points presented ❑
   d) To add colour ❑

8. When should you take questions?
   a) At the end ❑
   b) At the beginning ❑
   c) Take no questions ❑
   d) As arranged ahead of the start ❑

9. What's the best thing to do if you are asked a tricky question?
   a) Avoid the issue ❑
   b) Pause, think and give a considered answer ❑
   c) Blind people with jargon ❑
   d) Cast doubt on the questioner ❑

10. What's the purpose of speaker's notes?
    a) To remind you what to say ❑
    b) To remind you how to say it ❑
    c) To provide a framework for content and manner ❑
    d) No purpose – they should not be used ❑

FRIDAY

Follow-up action and the power of persistence

As we have seen, you're unlikely to maximize success in multi-stage selling without some good organizational skills and persistence. There is more to winning business than simply handling meetings in the right way and progressing from stage to stage until the client has satisfactorily gone through the processes they feel are necessary to making a decision.

Successful people recognize this fact and become adept at dealing with the follow-up action required. Today we investigate these skills, and what to do when:

- the client says yes
- the client wants to 'think about it'
- the client says no.

When the client says yes

Sometimes, after the presentation and the questions that may follow it, a firm decision one way or the other is made straight away. If agreement to your proposal is forthcoming, there are several things you need to do immediately.

First, it's good practice to couple your expression of thanks with (preferably specific) reassurance: 'Thanks very much; I'm sure you will find all this works out well.' Then consider any practical points that need to be dealt with at this stage:

- Is there documentation to be completed (guarantee, contract, service arrangement, etc.)?
- Do you need a signature?
- Is there information you need (invoice address, contacts, order number, delivery arrangements, etc.)?
- Are there points still to be discussed or agreed (such as delivery date)?

You must deal with all such matters in a prompt and businesslike way. You are still on show and it may still be possible for the client to change their mind or demand to negotiate more on price – something that could negate the result you think you've achieved. Deal with outstanding matters straight away and then end the meeting. Don't allow the meeting to descend into relaxed or idle chatter: many a person has talked themselves out of an order at this stage. Of course, some social chat may be important; there are deals where both parties regard lunch afterwards as natural. Just be a little wary.

If you are sure that the client – who no doubt values their time highly – really wants to extend the contact, decide on the objectives of such an extended meeting (it is surely part of or the start of a working relationship). Do you drop business, talk no 'shop' and treat it socially, or use it to move on to other topics? It is important to meet the client's needs in this respect. People will not like it if they planned to use the time constructively and you just talk of golf, or vice versa.

Once you have left the client, never fail to double-check that your internal paperwork is completed. It's easy to forget something vital – a figure or other detail – after a good lunch! When you have obtained agreement, the sales process may be at an end but ongoing sales activity to hold and develop the business further is just beginning.

When the client wants to 'think about it'

People may say a number of things rather than yes or no, and you may find that the most difficult thing to deal with is that little phrase, 'Let me think about it.' This is essentially positive, yet if you just walk away from it – helpfully allowing the client to do just that – then you may never speak to that person again. Some people who say this do actually mean no, but you will often need to take this response at face value.

The best reply may well be to agree with them; it is often difficult to think of a reason why the client should *not* think about it (unless perhaps you can give pressing reasons why they should decide at once). The best route is often not simply to agree but to urge the client to think about it. Tell them it is an important decision, tell them they must not make it lightly, and tell them they should not be rushed and that they must be certain. However you phrase it, make sure you are clearly on the side of thinking about it.

Use careful questioning

The next step is to ask them why exactly they still need to think about it, or what elements of the decision still need review. This is when your client may volunteer more information: perhaps there is a particular sticking point or they feel that something about the case has been less well argued than the rest, or that they need more information. Then you can try turning the intention back to more discussion, using careful questioning, as in the following example:

Client: 'Let me think about it.'
You: 'Of course, it's a big decision; you have to be sure.'
Client: 'That's right.'
You: 'You must be sure it's right in every respect. Is there any aspect which you need to think about particularly?'
Client: 'Well, I suppose it's the timescale that worries me most – it would be bound to affect current operations.'
You: 'To some extent that's true, but we can minimize that. Perhaps I didn't explain how we would approach that sufficiently. Can I go over it again before we finish?'
Client: 'Okay. I do want to have it all clear in my mind.'

Then the meeting is under way again. It may be that more than one point needs clarification but, that done, there is no reason why discussion cannot move on towards a positive conclusion.

There is an alternative here, however. The client may ask for time to think about it not because they need time to think, but for some other reason. Perhaps the two most likely are:

1 they need to confer with others in the organization or round the table to which you have just presented

2 they have a meeting planned with a competitor for comparative purposes.

In this case, careful questioning may discover the reason.

As a result of this new knowledge, the action on which you plan to close may change; for example, you might try to ensure that you get a further hearing after the competitor meeting. Again, the better the information you find out at every stage, the better position you are in to take things further. Such techniques are not infallible, but if they increase your strike rate even a little they are well worth pursuing, and you may be surprised by how often 'Let me think about it' leads, not to thinking about it, but to extended discussion and a positive decision.

Follow through on the agreement
When you do get agreement, remember that the quality of what you do next in working with or delivering to the client must be excellent. Delivering – with a capital D – is a prime factor in deciding whether more business will result in future.

If you have to wait for a decision after your formal pitch, maintain the initiative by keeping in touch or arranging the next contact. Don't just let them leave, saying 'We'll let you know.' Indeed, there is an old saying that when people say 'We'll let you know' – you know!

Arrange the next contact

You can act to try to arrange the next contact. You can either ask: 'Can we get together again once you've considered further – when will that be?' or 'Can I suggest we meet again once you've considered further – what about one day early next week?' Whatever the route, the objective is to have specific agreement to a dated and timed further meeting (or whatever the next contact needs to be) before you walk out of the door.

You will not always succeed, but when you do that removes the need to follow up later, something which may be more awkward. If things are going well, if the client has liked everything done to date, why not move on one more step and get them to agree the date of another meeting – all while they are in the mood to say yes?

If that's not possible, you'll need to find other ways of driving the process forward.

Stay in touch

If follow-up dates have not been firmly agreed, your job is to stay in touch with the client and let them know that you have not gone away. Remember that, if you allow a long gap, perhaps out of embarrassment (it is difficult to chase further if you have phoned three times and always been told they are in a meeting), you may be allowing more persistent competitors to sneak in. Don't overdo the frequency of contact, however; understand that the time going by is not necessarily negative – they no doubt have other things than you to worry about– but keep the pot boiling, as it were.

Ring the changes, too, in terms of method:

- **Phone** them, but remember you can't see what is happening at the other end – it may be a bad moment that gets you a brush-off.
- **Write** to them, for example a letter thanking them for the opportunity to present, reinforcing benefits and referring to details of follow-up that may have been agreed. This will bridge a gap and may be appreciated.
- **Email**, but do not overdo it. Even though this is often seen as the easiest way to communicate, you still need to make sure your emails are well written. Remember that emails take only a split second to delete.

If you've carried out a number of conventional follow-up contacts without success, a less routine approach might be called for. If a more creative method of attracting your prospect's attention seems appropriate, this needs care but can be memorable and win business. Don't reject anything other than the conventional formal approach; try a little experiment with non-business language and see what it can do for you. See the box below for an example of this.

Creative follow-up: an example

After writing a short book for a specialist publisher, I was keen to undertake another topic for them in the same format. My proposal got a generally good reaction but no confirmation. I wrote and telephoned many times but always received a less than positive response. I wanted to try again but all the conventional possibilities seemed exhausted. Finally, I decided to send the following message:

'**Struggling author**, patient, reliable (non-smoker), seeks commission on business topics. Novel formats preferred, but anything considered within reason. Ideally 100 or so pages on a topic like sales excellence sounds good, maybe with some illustrations. Delivery of the right quantity of material – on time – guaranteed. Contact me at the above address/telephone number or meet on neutral ground, carrying a copy of *Publishing News* and wearing a carnation.'

Despite some hesitation, wondering if this was over the top (it was to someone I had met only once), I sent it. Gratifyingly, confirmation came the following day, and the result was publication of *The Sales Excellence Pocketbook*.

Persistence helps win business and you will get to a decision in due course; certainly, never regard something as lost until you have been told so. It is a pity to lose touch just because you fail to understand what is delaying matters and then find you are thought of as having lost interest.

When the client says no

It's a shame if this happens and it must prompt two actions:

- **Analysing why:** a postmortem is no fun but may well help you do better next time. It is particularly difficult to contact the person who has declined and ask why, but this may be useful or even game-changing (and I have known decisions be reversed following such a call)
- **Looking ahead:** if they are not going to be a client today, maybe they can be in future.

Look ahead: arrange for a carefully organized series of contacts to be systematically and rigorously carried out; make sure someone has this responsibility. Keeping in touch with your failed prospect can still lead to future business. The largest single order I ever received came after a small job for a client was followed by two full years when I did nothing for them and during which I contacted the decision maker eight times (a mixed series of contacts involving one chance meeting). When a new order came I blessed my resolve at maintaining contact; my actions took a little time and effort but acted positively on the client and kept me in mind.

Summary

The moral here is clear. A good deal of time, effort and money has been put in to get any prospect to the point where proposals have been submitted and a presentation has been made. Things cannot be left there.

A considered response needs to be made to the specific circumstances pertaining at the end of the presentation. You need to maintain contact that is of an acceptable type and frequency to your prospective client. Taking the initiative and continuing this process of maintaining contact are important, even given ultimate success in your pitch, because it will then be more likely that you'll be successful in the future, in terms of gaining new, repeat and ongoing business.

It is possible to sum up today's message in two words: be persistent.

SUNDAY

MONDAY

TUESDAY

WEDNESDAY

THURSDAY

FRIDAY

SATURDAY

Fact-check [answers at the back]

1. What should you do if your prospect requests time to think about your pitch?
   a) Panic ❑
   b) Launch back into your case ❑
   c) Just wait ❑
   d) Agree, and ask why ❑

2. How long should you wait for a decision?
   a) A day ❑
   b) A week ❑
   c) An *agreed* time ❑
   d) A month ❑

3. What's the first thing to do if they say yes?
   a) Punch the air ❑
   b) Order champagne ❑
   c) Say thank you ❑
   d) Tell your colleagues 'I got it!' ❑

4. When persistent follow-up is necessary, what should you do?
   a) Send the same note repeatedly ❑
   b) Do nothing but telephone ❑
   c) Be systematic and creative ❑
   d) Give up ❑

5. When agreement is reached, what should you do?
   a) Check and deal with the resulting paperwork ❑
   b) End the meeting instantly ❑
   c) Move on to social chat ❑
   d) Report back to the office ❑

6. If a successful meeting moves into lunch, what should you do?
   a) Move talk away from business ❑
   b) Tell funny jokes ❑
   c) Follow the client's lead ❑
   d) Get drunk ❑

7. What should you do if the prospect's final answer is no?
   a) Never speak to them again ❑
   b) Tell them they're making a bad decision ❑
   c) Storm out in umbrage ❑
   d) Commence action to make them a client in future ❑

8. What prime characteristic do you need to make follow-up successful?
   a) Indifference ❑
   b) Persistence ❑
   c) Humility ❑
   d) Shyness ❑

SATURDAY

Creating and maintaining a high strike rate

Now that you have learned about all the main stages of the pitching process, you'll understand that there is no magic formula for success. To a large degree, success is in the detail. It is also evident that success lies with the individual.

Of course, products and services vary and the quality and value for money they offer helps people decide to buy. But so, too, does the way you and your colleagues present yourselves. How you behave at every stage has a powerful part to play in the process and will seem indicative of the service and performance to follow. The prospective client will frequently differentiate your offer from your competitors' on the basis of your style of pitch, and thus it is you – and your colleagues – who can make the difference between success and failure.

Today you will learn how to build on and strengthen your skills at pitching as you take things forward. You'll also read some handy dos and don'ts for focusing your activity in the right way.

Taking things forward

Here are a number of things you can do to help build and strengthen the pitching process.

● **Keep records of the conversion rate**
On average, how many people do you have to see to get the opportunity to pitch? How many let you put in proposals but do not take things further? With what proportion do you secure business? How many offer repeat opportunities, and for how long? Your rate of strike may surprise you and acting to improve it at any stage will directly affect both productivity and profit.

● **Experiment**
Vary your methods a little and see how this affects things. Do longer or shorter proposal documents work best? Work out why some people are more likely to win business than others. Use your analysis to inform your own approach.

● **Be honest**
The pitching process demands not only a number of skills but also a high order of them. For example, you must not only be able to write in a way that is grammatical but in a way that is clear, descriptive, memorable and, from your point of view, persuasive. If you or others involved in the process are lacking in any way, then take action, undertaking some training

perhaps. Practice will help, and so too will analysing how things go and focusing on understanding the reasons for an outcome. This means looking at both successes and failures: you can repeat and extend the things that work and avoid or correct a technique that fails to do its job.

Review regularly
This is an ongoing process, during which you review the success rate, your people skills and also the experiences you have of making pitches. Compare notes with colleagues and consider canvassing those to whom you present, successfully or not, for their opinion of how you rate.

Give it enough time
Despite other pressures, making a good pitch cannot be rushed. It needs thought, it may need research and collaboration, and it will certainly take time to prepare and execute well. Writing a good proposal, for example, may take a while and, even when executed with care, is best slept on and reviewed the next day; very few good ones do not go through some editing before they are sent to the client.

Check everything
Some organizations make it mandatory for all proposals to be read by someone other than their author before they are sent. Such a practice provides a safety net and makes it likely that more business is won than lost. An extra pair of eyes looking over a document can make it more likely that simple mistakes will not be missed; for example, one proposal was lost primarily because the word 'dairy' in the client company's name was spelt 'diary'. Be warned!

Keep the process fresh
Elements of pitching are by their nature repetitive. Perhaps every proposal you write covers similar topics. Even something as basic as a clear description of your organization – something you could no doubt wax lyrical about at length but which must be encapsulated succinctly – can become stale. Such things need refreshing, not to create change for the sake of change but to ensure that everything is being stated in the best possible way.

● **Avoid the standard**
By its nature, the sort of sales situation described here demands a bespoke approach. A pitch should not say 'This is what we do for people'; it should say 'This is what we recommend we do for you.' This sense of being treated as a unique entity should always be apparent to the client at every stage of the process.

● **Don't forget the 'human' aspect**
Of course, facts win business, but the human or emotional content of a pitch is also important: it can be the final weight on one side of the balance that tips the decision in your direction. If the client is faced with two very similar offers (which happens surprisingly often), they may opt simply for the people they like best, who seem the most trustworthy, professional and expert. All these qualities – professionalism, enthusiasm, interest and empathy, experience and expertise – must shine through.

Dos and don'ts

The following checklist of dos and don'ts recaps much of the information we have covered this week. Use it as a handy reference for when you need a reminder of how to focus your activity in the right way.

Do:	
• concentrate on the facts	The case you put over must be credible and factual. A clear-cut 'these are all the facts you need to know' approach tends to pay particular dividends.
• use repetition	Key points can appear more than once, for example in the proposal and in the presentation, and even more than once within one of these. This applies, of course, especially to benefits repeated for emphasis.
• keep changing the language	You need to find different ways of saying the same thing to avoid verbatim repetition, being contrived and boring your audience.
• say what's new	If you have something new, novel or even unique to say, make sure people know it. Take care to differentiate your offer from your competitors', and make your key points stand out.
• address the client/prospect	Do this accurately and precisely. You must know exactly whom you are addressing, what their needs, likes and dislikes are and be ever conscious of tailoring the message. Going too far towards being all things to all people will dilute the effectiveness of your message with respect to any one individual or organization.
• keep them reading your proposals	With written proposals, consider breaking sentences at the end of a page so that readers have to turn over to complete the sentence. (Yes, it does look less neat, but it works.) Always make it clear that other pages follow, putting 'continued...' or similar at the foot of the page.
• link paragraphs	This is another way to keep them reading (or listening). Use 'horse and cart' points to carry the argument along. For example, start one paragraph with 'One example of this is...' and the next with 'Now let's look at how that works...'
• be descriptive	For example, describe a system as 'as smooth as silk' rather than as 'very straightforward to operate'. Remember, you know how good what you are describing is; your audience does not. You need to tell them and you must not assume they will catch your enthusiasm from a brief phrase: explain it.
• involve people	When mentioning your colleagues, give their names: say 'John Smith, the head of our XYZ division, will...', not merely 'the head of our XYZ division will...' And when mentioning other people, say 'More than 300 clients have found it valuable', not merely 'It is a proven service.'

• add credibility	For example, if you quote users, give their names (with their permission); if you quote numbers/statistics, quote them specifically; and if you mention people, do so by name. Being specific adds to your credibility, so saying 'This is described on page 16 of our brochure...' is better than simply 'This is described in our brochure...'

Don't:

• be too clever	It's the argument that should win people round, not your flowery phrases, elegant quotations or clever approach.
• be too complicated	The point about simplicity has been made. It applies equally to the overall argument.
• be pompous	This means saying too much about you, your organization and your product/services (instead of what it means to others). It means communicating in a way that is too far removed from the way you would speak. It means following too slavishly the 'correct' grammar at the expense of an easy, flowing style.
• overclaim	While you should certainly have the courage of your convictions, too many superlatives can become self-defeating. Make one claim that seems doubtful and your whole argument will suffer.
• offer opinions	It's more important to offer facts – ideally facts you can substantiate.
• lead into points with negatives	Instead of saying, for example, 'If this is not the case we will...' say 'You will find...or...'
• assume people lack knowledge	Rather than saying, for example, 'You probably don't know that...' say 'Many people have not yet heard...' or 'Like others, you probably know...'
• overdo humour	Never use humour unless you are sure of success. An inward groan from your prospect will destroy the nodding agreement you are trying to build. A witty quotation or quip, if relevant, is safer and, even if its humour is not appreciated, the appropriateness of its content may make a point.
• use up benefits early	A persuasive message must not run out of steam: it must end on a high note and still be couched in terms of benefits even towards and at the end of the pitch.

Summary

What all the points described today add up to is an attitude, and an important one at that. Beyond the skills, the techniques and tactics you have learned this week, it's very much *how* you think about and approach the pitching process that matters. Some good luck along the way may help, but you cannot, must not, rely on it.

It is the way you manage and execute the process that will decide your success. Rarely do people succeed in winging it. You are the element, above all, that creates successful pitches and you *can* make them happen; all you need is a careful, systematic approach that is applied with confidence and flair.

Go for it; tomorrow a new week begins.

SUNDAY

MONDAY

TUESDAY

WEDNESDAY

THURSDAY

FRIDAY

SATURDAY

Fact-check [answers at the back]

1. What record kept can most readily prompt improved pitching success?
   a) Strike rate ❏
   b) Sales volume ❏
   c) Product mix ❏
   d) Order size ❏

2. What approach is best for a new pitch?
   a) Sticking with the historic method ❏
   b) Experimenting and adapting ❏
   c) Making random changes ❏
   d) Basing the approach on the last ❏

3. If your skills lag behind the need for them, what should you do?
   a) Delegate pitches to someone else ❏
   b) Just hope practice will improve them ❏
   c) Take specific (developmental) action ❏
   d) Muddle through regardless ❏

4. How often should you review the pitching process?
   a) Occasionally ❏
   b) As regularly as is practically possible ❏
   c) Never ❏
   d) Annually ❏

5. How much time should you give to preparing the pitch?
   a) One hour ❏
   b) Five hours ❏
   c) One day ❏
   d) As much as it takes ❏

6. How should you keep all your descriptions?
   a) Rigid ❏
   b) Fresh ❏
   c) Repetitive ❏
   d) Flowery ❏

7. What must the final form of what you do reflect?
   a) A typical client ❏
   b) Past clients ❏
   c) Non-clients ❏
   d) This particular client ❏

8. Which of the following is most important to a successful pitch?
   a) Tangible aspects ❏
   b) Intangible aspects ❏
   c) Both tangible and intangible aspects ❏
   d) Neither aspect ❏

Surviving in tough times

Here's a safe prediction: the future looks like being uncertain. This is hardly helpful, but we all know that recent times have been difficult – the banks, the economy, the euro and more. The result is recession and low growth and firm forecasts that the situation will take some years to improve. Clearly, waiting for things to 'get back to normal' is simply not an option. In pitching for business, all this makes things likely to be more difficult than they would be in other circumstances. This section offers ten key points that may help maintain the possibility of success despite difficult times. Indeed, in one respect such times represent an opportunity. The key word here is competitiveness.

1 Assume that competition exists

Always assume that a prospect is talking to others (and ask about it). Include the implications of this in your thinking and your presentation, and remember that it is perfectly possible for a good presentation about what is actually a less good solution to beat a poorly presented pitch about a good solution. It may not be 'fair' but it is so.

2 Build on success

It's always easier to sell to an existing or past customer than to find and persuade a new one, so maintain good communications and good relations with all your existing and past clients. Make suggestions about future work and if – when – the opportunity arises to pitch for something new, allow no dilution in what you do to occur 'because they know us so well'; pitch to them as well as you possibly can.

3 Make all pitches perfect pitches

This is a simple point but worth emphasizing: it's never easy to get a pitch just right, and any weakness, any lack of attention, can dilute its effectiveness. In troubled times you simply need to leave no stone unturned in your quest to make every one excellent: this means taking more care, doing more checking, and increasing your creativity.

4 Create and build skills

If you cannot make your pitches excellent – or some of your colleagues involved cannot – due to any, even modest, shortfall in skill (the ability to write or present well enough, for instance), then such skills must be studied, developed and fine-tuned. This is not something that can be put off; reading this book is a useful start.

5 Prepare properly

It takes time – there are other tasks and other pressures – but don't 'wing it'. Get ready, think it through and plan thoroughly – and this applies to all those involved. If you take short cuts, you run the risk of missing something that turns out to be vital to success. There is only one 'magic ingredient' that can create winning pitches for you – it is you and how you go about the whole process.

6 Use language to produce clarity

Effective communication is often difficult and yet it is a vital ingredient when pitching. No one will agree to a proposal or buy anything that they don't fully understand. True clarity – perhaps

unexpected clarity – scores points, and in challenging times it is
something on which to concentrate.

7 Add power to your descriptions

You must avoid the bland. Good description of technical
matters, or anything else, must paint a picture. I once heard
something described as being as slippery as a freshly buttered
ice rink. That's surely unmistakably slippery; that's really
descriptive and a good example of how an original simile can
lift your descriptions and make them memorable.

8 Link to careful pricing policy

Perhaps this goes a little beyond our brief here, but price,
cost-effectiveness and value for money rate high among the
reasons to buy. This aspect of what you pitch must be well
thought through and matched to your proposal. The cheapest
product or service is neither always wanted nor always bought,
but things must be costed right and value sold hard.

9 Be persistent

It's difficult to get a book published and it is rightly said that
writers with no persistence can be described with one word –
unpublished. This is true in many other areas, too: following
up, staying in touch and not letting business be lost by default
are all part of creating a high strike rate.

10 Differentiate

Pitches can be won or lost by a whisker. Small details can
make or break them, so everything that differentiates you
from others in troubled times can aid success. Make every
description, every approach and the very manner in which
you do things work to differentiate you, to make you seem
extra professional and extra credible and what you have to say
irresistible. You and your organization are unique, so make
sure your pitches make that clear and you can win business
even in troubled times.

Answers

Sunday: 1b; 2c; 3c; 4c; 5a; 6c; 7a; 8c; 9b; 10a.

Monday: 1c; 2a; 3b; 4d; 5c; 6d; 7c; 8b.

Tuesday: 1c; 2c; 3d; 4c; 5d; 6d; 7b; 8d; 9d; 10c.

Wednesday: 1b; 2d; 3c; 4d; 5d; 6a; 7d; 8c.

Thursday: 1d; 2c; 3c; 4b; 5b; 6b; 7c; 8d; 9b; 10c.

Friday: 1d; 2c; 3c; 4c; 5a; 6c; 7d; 8b.

Saturday: 1a; 2b; 3c; 4b; 5d; 6b; 7d; 8c.

Further reading

Forsyth, P., *How to Write Reports and Proposals* (London: Kogan Page, 2013)

Forsyth, P., *The PowerPoint Detox* (London: Kogan Page, 2009)

Forsyth, P., *The Sales Excellence Pocketbook* (Alresford: Management Pocketbooks, 1998)

Harvey, C., *Successful Selling* (London: Hodder, Teach Yourself, 2012)

Kay, F. and Kite, N., *Understanding NLP – strategies for better workplace communication, without the jargon* (London: Kogan Page, 2009)

Lapworth, K., *The Writer's Guide to Good Style* (London: Hodder, Teach Yourself, 2012)

Oulten, N.B., *Killer Presentations* (Oxford: How to Books, 2007)